THE JOURNEY TO
CALM

THE JOURNEY TO
CALM

A Perfectionist's Guide to Letting Up, Slowing Down and Finding Peace

DEBBIE FRAKES

Copyright © 2021 by Debbie Frakes.
All rights reserved.

Cataloging-in-Publication Data is on file with the Library of Congress.
ISBN: 978-1-7370805-0-3
Ebook ISBN: 978-1-7370805-1-0
Library of Congress Control Number: 2021908713

Design by Amy Hayes Design
Editorial production by kn literary

Printed in the United States of America

10 9 8 7 6 5 4 3 2 1

*To my younger self — of all ages —
for all you experienced to
make me who I am today.
I am beyond grateful to you.*

Contents

INTRODUCTION 9

PART ONE: CONSCIOUSNESS 15

    Chapter One: Cultivating Awareness 17
    Chapter Two: Becoming the Observer 27
    Chapter Three: Taking a Pause 37

PART TWO: ACTION 45

    Chapter Four: Changing the Story 47
    Chapter Five: Trusting Your Intuition 59
    Chapter Six: Asking for Help 71

PART THREE: LETTING GO 79

    Chapter Seven: Accepting What Is 81
    Chapter Eight: Surrendering and Letting Go 93
    Chapter Nine: Trusting That
        Something Better Is Coming 103

PART FOUR: MAINTENANCE 113

    Chapter Ten: Continuing the CALM Journey 115

ENDNOTES 117

ACKNOWLEDGMENTS 119

ABOUT THE AUTHOR 121

Introduction

This is a little book of life lessons that I wish I could send back in time to my younger self. I may not be able to reach that little girl who felt broken and unworthy, but I hope that I can inspire someone who needs it.

You're going to find wisdom in this book and how I came to learn it. But that wisdom—through these lessons—doesn't come from my being uniquely enlightened. Instead, it comes from what I've overcome and what I continue to work on.

This journey to wisdom is a lifelong one, and my experience is only one version. Yet we struggle with many of the same patterns, beliefs and behaviors. These universal challenges keep us from leading a calm and peaceful life, regardless of when we learned them, what we label them or why we don't let go of them.

I was bullied in school for being smart, shy and unattractive—the trifecta of personal shame. I would have given just about anything to be liked—heck, even just accepted—by the kids I deemed worthy (read: popular). When I wasn't, I internalized the shame, and internalized it so deeply that even when their voices faded into the past, the critical internal voice inside my head remained strong, reproaching me that I simply wasn't enough unless I performed flawlessly, was attractive, charming, sexy, successful and admired. (And even when I was those things, that sneaky, spiteful voice still told me I wasn't enough.)

So, I set off on a lifelong journey to find "enough." It became my passion and my life's work, starting when I was about thirteen years old. I began dieting, even though I had no need to, and my austere food restrictions set me up for a lifetime of eating issues. I was reading Norman Vincent Peale at fourteen, Leo Buscaglia and Wayne Dyer a year later. I was a self-admitted self-improvement junkie, sure that I would find the key to being enough in the next book.

For decades, I followed some kind of crazy treasure map, searching outside myself for self-love and enoughness. I tried just about everything—self-help books (I could start a library), dieting, makeovers, paychecks, promotions, clothing, exercising, religion, gourmet cooking, wine connoisseurship and on and on. And except for some insights provided by the self-help books, the other things provided nothing other than fleeting satisfaction—and even then, it wasn't by making me the best version I could be, it was the illusion that I was better than others. Temporarily.

My identity defined success as the rate of my climb up the corporate ladder, my salary, bonus, number of frequent-flier miles, international travel, public and private praise from leaders, encounters with the rich and famous and being the resident wine snob. And if any of these things were suddenly on shaky ground, then my identity, self-confidence and self-worth wobbled right with them.

That illustrates the perfectionism I still struggle with today. When I couldn't be perfect or the best, it meant I wasn't worthy. This set up a visceral need to control people, situations and outcomes, which led to a lifetime of unmet expectations: a failure on my part to manage the world.

So, I tried harder, and when that didn't work, I turned to less healthy vehicles to "manage" or eliminate the anxiety, fear and failure.

In high school and college, I looked for my "enough" in food and the desperate need for approval. After college, it was relationships and the desperate need for approval. Then it was a career and success—and the desperate need for approval. And then, a few more years down the road, wine, and yes, the desperate need for approval. But the bottom line to all these things was the feeling—no, the unerring belief—that something was missing, and whatever it was, it was outside of me.

Where do you find your worthiness? Is it in your business card or job title? Is it in your children's or spouse's accomplishments? Your accomplishments? The size of your home or how many homes you have? The kind of car you drive or the brand of purse you carry? Or is it found somewhere in your core, in that still, silent foundational place where you know you're enough, no matter what?

Most of us are generally in the former camp, although if you've ever touched hearts with that inner knowing, you realize the job title, salary, bonus, square footage or purse logo are, in the end, empty. And you can't fill up empty with empty.

For years, I tried patching my low self-worth by using these things. I also tried all manner of self-improvement books, which helped some more, but came up woefully short when the Perfectionist was overwhelmed at work, didn't do every role, assignment or event perfectly and internalized every near miss as a failure. The pressure of an increasingly stressful career could be overwhelming enough. The pressure I put on myself was unbearable. And my search for something to relieve this pressure and fill up the emptiness ended up in wine.

I can't tell you the exact point when wine went from a hobby to a habit, or from a habit to an addiction. And that the life I had planned on—climbing to the pinnacle of the corporate ladder, having my income climb right with it, being lauded for my skills and talents, buying a vineyard and retiring to become a winemaker—all evaporated, and rather quickly.

To quote the old Yiddish saying, "Man plans. God laughs." I imagine God certainly was giggling over what I thought would be a fulfilling life.

There was something far better in store for me. But at the time, I was utterly without hope that things could get better. I didn't care if I lived. I didn't care if I died. I just didn't care. Period.

"How did I get here?" I asked myself often. It was at that point, beyond not caring, that I somehow mustered enough courage to ask a more important question: "How can I pack up and move out?"

I've been in recovery more than a decade—and they've been the most amazing, fulfilling years of my life. Beyond a program that keeps me sober, I've restored myself through personal growth, coaching, yoga and trying to connect with that all-wise higher self.

In the process, I've learned that addiction was just one more manifestation of my search for enoughness. When I stopped drinking wine, all the reasons I drank in the first place didn't go away. Recovery from one required recovery from the other. And they had to happen simultaneously.

This is a book about recovery—not in the traditional sense, but recovery from the patterns and stories that no longer serve our highest good. These patterns and stories are addictions in their own right: they run without our conscious permission, get stronger with time and, in many cases, keep us hopeless and miserable. And we tend to run from what makes us uncomfortable—people, situations, interactions, places.

This book is my journey of healing—of lessons that I've learned—that follows four phases of growth: Consciousness, Action, Letting Go and Maintenance (CALM).

Consciousness. Any major life change begins with a conscious decision to change. We decide that our way isn't working. We become aware not just of our thoughts, patterns and reactions, but also of our ability to separate from them.

Action. We often believe we have one choice: react. But we have many choices when it comes to responding to challenging situations and emotions—choices that move us in the direction of growth and bring us more clarity and peace.

Letting go. Perhaps the most difficult of the steps, especially for us fiercely independent souls. At some point, though, we find that no matter how hard we try, we can't fix things. So, learning to lean on something other than yourself—whatever you might call it—can work miracles.

Maintenance. This is the conditioning phase, because these are not one-off situations. Emotions and challenges aren't one-and-done. But the good news is that each time they reoccur, we're stronger and more capable of dealing with them.

Each chapter also includes a letter to my younger self—with the loving wisdom I wish I would have known at the time.

These lessons and letters most certainly would have brought peace, clarity and strength to that shy, sensitive soul who never felt worthy. This book is my gift to my younger self and to you. May it serve you well, wherever you are on your journey.

PART ONE
Consciousness

CHAPTER ONE

Cultivating Awareness

I was standing in an exam room with my family doctor and my husband. My doctor was quietly but firmly advising me of how my drinking was impacting my body. I was feeling cornered; it was two against one, and I didn't want to hear anything about how I needed to stop drinking wine. But at one point during the discussion, I became acutely present and aware, sensed a presence behind me and felt, not heard, the words, *It's time to ask for help.*

It was a moment of strong, divine intuition, and I said, "Yes." It wasn't a resounding yes. It wasn't a yes full of acceptance and surrender. Those would come later. But it was a pinprick of willingness.

Any one of a million behaviors can bring us to this precipice of change. But for me, alcohol just did it more swiftly and harshly than anything else had.

Perhaps it's the wounded look on your children's faces when you lose your temper yet again over lost lunch money. Perhaps it's a growing hopelessness over going to work at a job that seems to suck the soul out of you every day. Perhaps it's going from one painful, abusive relationship to another, looking for validation.

And then you get to a point where you've had enough. Where a small sliver of sunlight breaks through your delusion and reminds you that you're not permanently trapped in your patterns—that there is hope in growth.

Oh, taking that first step is hard. Just like the hardest part of yoga is putting on your leggings. All the voices—fear, shame, judging—start crowing and croaking for homeostasis, to keep you stuck. They're afraid too. But ultimately, these patterns, these stories, crimp the line—the flow of abundance and joy.

The soul may speak softly, but it is strong, and if you listen hard enough to its whisperings, it will guide you.

When faced with a difficult emotion or situation, it's natural to want to do something to get rid of the feeling. Fight or flight are survival instincts hardwired into the reptilian portion of our brain. They were critical to our ancestors who were often faced with a saber-toothed tiger looking for a snack. But today, when the saber-toothed tiger has morphed into a saber-toothed boss or a difficult relationship or an eighty-hour workweek, then I think there needs to be a third response: look the difficulty right in the eye and work through it.

Indeed, painful situations often do require action (in my case, giving up wine), but action without contemplation is not generally the best answer, so the first thing we need to do is become conscious.

There's a saying in recovery communities that your drinking isn't the problem, your thinking is the problem. True. But until you decide to get rid of the alcohol or the drugs or whatever demon is driving your bus, it's difficult, if not downright impossible, to mend your thinking. Once you do, you can get to work in earnest.

And that all starts with consciously choosing to become aware of and watch your mind do its thing. Our brains are amazing and beautiful. They allow love, creation, compassion, imagination and inspiration. But they also are hardwired for our survival, because of that fight-or-flight instinct that thousands of years ago kept us safe from saber-toothed tigers. Today, that instinct lives on.

Our reactions, whether physical, mental or emotional, are learned. We pick them up from parents, siblings, teachers, friends. And we strengthen them.

Let's say the same stimulus triggers you repeatedly. Perhaps it started with the bully in fifth grade who tormented you about your looks and shamed you for being ugly. You respond by internalizing his comments ("I am worthless") and becoming submissive whenever you see him, even going so far as to try to do something, anything, to please him and get him off your back.

Then, decades later, enter an aggressive coworker who makes a sarcastic comment about your outfit. You're immediately triggered. In a millisecond, your brain overlays the bully's face on your coworker's, and you immediately go into submissive, people-pleasing mode, instead of responding in a more self-affirming way.

Think about the voices you've internalized through the years. You know the ones. It's like your own inner critic committee—the group that holds wild parties in your head, starts food fights and generally tries to unseat your serenity and centeredness.

Here's my own cast of characters, who may have made guest appearances in your head as well.

Fear. The leader of the pack, the alpha dog who wears a creepy monster mask. With one evil look from fear, we feel that visceral sensation of not being safe, not being secure, and believe there's indeed a monster under the bed (even when it's really just dust bunnies).

The Evil Storyteller. An all-too-familiar voice (think Vincent Price meets the Wicked Witch of the West) whose repertoire is nothing but depressing, frightening stories that keep us stuck.

The Chief Critic and Judge. She revels in pointing out our latest wrinkle (literal or figurative), flaw or faux pas. Her favorite words are should and shouldn't, and she's quick to cite case law (a.k.a. past transgressions) as irrefutable evidence of unworthiness.

The Skeptic. Always quick to dose our dreams with doubt: "Are you sure you can do that?" "You've never done that before." "You're not qualified."

The Perfectionist. A study in two extremes: either inaction ("You'd better not try this because you won't be good at it.") or perpetual action. ("Just a little more tweaking and it will be done. Oh, wait, here's another spot you missed.") Both are aimed at acquiring external approval. (She, by the way, made a number of guest appearances as I was writing this book.)

The Drama Queen. Always ready to give an Oscar-winning performance on making Mt. Fuji out of a speed bump.

Anxiety. Constantly worrying about what's going to happen tomorrow, next month or next year, and scheming about how she can control it and keep it from happening.

Depression. The one I secretly call Eeyore, who slumps in, shoulders and head down, and mumbles, "The sky has fallen. Always knew it would."

They're uncomfortable emotions, no doubt. So, what do you do when they decide to hold an impromptu meeting or food fight? The first thought that comes to mind is to bind and gag them, heave them into a really dark part of your psyche and pretend they're not there. But shutting the door on them doesn't work. The feelings will sit on the doorstep, or hide around the corner, or just stand there, ringing the doorbell like pesky trick-or-treaters until you answer the door. Inviting them in and telling them they can stay indefinitely in the spare bedroom doesn't work. They'll drive you crazy, and the longer you hang on to them, the harder it is to get rid of them.

Most of us will try in some way to escape them, run a mental marathon in the opposite direction. Choose your escape pod: shopping, drinking, drugging, anything that makes you forget your problems.

Unfortunately, they'll still be there after you've maxed out your department store credit card or woken up with the nastiest hangover of the twenty-first century.

Even if you think you've successfully locked them up for good, they'll find a way to escape. It may not be tomorrow or next week. But one day, when you're puttering around peacefully, they'll make a jailbreak. And like any negative thought, they will have grown stronger in the darkness of denial.

Importantly, it's not just mental chatter that goes on here. Strong emotions and thoughts trigger a physical response. Your amygdala—that ancient part of your brain that controls your fight-or-flight response—hears "danger" and releases hormones like cortisol and adrenaline. Enter the anxious, shaky feeling and the burning sensation in your solar plexus.

So, what do we do? Are we destined to just slither through life, reacting to stimuli with our reptilian brain calling the shots? Heavens, no. But where we get in trouble is listening to that primitive part of our brain that says, "Act and act now! Do something! Get rid of this horrible, uncomfortable feeling/emotion."

The only way to deal with these emotions once and for all is to feel them. To let them move through us. Sometimes, we will need to take some sort of action, but the first step is just to be aware of what we're feeling.

We need to learn that we are not our mind. Its little tricks and patterns develop just like any part of our physical bodies. This is hard to wrap your head around, because when you're anxious or depressed, it feels as much a part of you as your arm or your eyes. It feels like you are the anxiety. I know because I've been there—and I still visit. However, when we think we are the feeling, especially the strong ones, our fight-or-flight instinct kicks in and triggers all sorts of coping behaviors, like shopping, drinking, drugging, lashing out at people.

Making a conscious choice to face our discomfort can be difficult; but it's not impossible. Otherwise, those suffering from trauma would never heal, those who were verbally abused would never believe they were worthy, those who never received any love would never love. Yet they do.

Here are a couple of tools I've used to become more aware in the midst of mental discomfort.

Acknowledge the way you're feeling. Sometimes, just a nod toward the strong emotion (for example, "I'm feeling depression right now.") is enough to deflate it a bit—remove some of the power it has over you. And always try to acknowledge without judgment—don't label it a "good" or a "bad" feeling. Sometimes an emotion just wants to be noticed, and then it will slip away like Carl Sandburg's fog on cat's feet.

Try to identify it. If you feel anxious, where do you feel it? Is it in your head? Your stomach? Does it have a color? A shape? Does it change shapes? For me, depression feels like ten dental X-ray aprons stacked on my chest. Smothering. Immovable. Gray. Your feeling might also look like an animal or a person, maybe a parent, or a younger version of yourself. The point is, it's a construct of your mind not an intrinsic part of who you are.

Get curious. You can ask the emotion, "Why are you here?" to try and discern the lesson it might be carrying or what it really is. Anger is a common mask for grief. Depression a mask for boredom. Anxiety a mask for fear.

Make a date—for another time. Tell the emotion, "I hear you. Let's talk tomorrow, okay?" When you hear the familiar voices piping up (for me, anxiety gets very loud when I'm trying to go to sleep), this response may bring some relief. You're not denying the feelings or thoughts, just asking for a brief respite.

Play, even if the last thing you feel like doing is playing. "Wanna dance?" "Do some karaoke?" I don't know about you, but the idea of fox-trotting with Fear or singing "I Got You Babe" with Depression is enough to make me giggle. And sometimes a quick change of mental scenery (aka breaking your pattern) is enough for the emotions to hightail it for the door.

Think about your "why." Your "why" is the impetus that caused you to decide to change in the first place. One woman I know made her final decision to stop drinking when she was in the stall of a Catholic church restroom. Leaving her small kids alone at the pew, she had excused herself twice during the service to go drink from the miniature Dewar's bottles stashed in her purse. As she finished her third little bottle on the toilet, she was hit with an overwhelming sensation of, *No more. Enough. I don't want to lose my kids.* Now, when she's tempted to listen to the voice that tells her she doesn't have a drinking problem, she thinks of her kids sitting alone on the pew, and her resolve doesn't waver.

Becoming aware of what we're really feeling is not for the faint of heart. Our instinct will be to act, do something, run—anything to get rid of the emotions. But that's the very behavior that gets us in trouble. Plus, it's like feeding the emotions spinach and Cream of Wheat, topped with kale and protein powder: they just get stronger with our denial.

Awareness is key to understanding what's going on in the haunted house that is our heads. In addition to becoming aware of what you're feeling—anger, anxiety, boredom, depression—become aware of your resistance to it, because it's the resistance—the big no—that gets us in trouble.

Without awareness, we don't know what's really going on. Behind the strong emotion, there very well may be a lesson.

If the Perfectionist has me running in circles, I need to become aware and remind myself that I'm perfectly enough, just as I am.

If Fear has me immobilized from taking action toward my dreams, I can remember my why, which is to follow my heart, hopefully inspiring others along the way.

If Depression has me feeling hopeless, I can make a small effort to say, "I love you, Depression, old friend," and then do something extra to take care of that sad part of myself.

If the Skeptic beleaguers me about not being qualified to write a book, I can remind her that, because I am the only me that exists, no one else has the same perspective and experiences.

A letter to my twelve-year-old self

This is a note from your wiser, future self to help you understand how special you are, how it's essential to trust your path and, most importantly, how to love who you are in every moment.

You will encounter kids who make fun of you and call you ugly and "the brain." Acknowledge that their words hurt your tender heart, then stand in front of a mirror and declare that you're beautiful and smart and will do amazing things.

You will read Teen magazine and compare yourself to other girls and feel unworthy because you don't have long blonde hair or tan easily. Know that those things cease to matter sooner than you think. And understand that you are the only one of you in the Universe, and that alone makes you very special and worthy.

You will worry about and exert massive effort to control your appearance, other peoples' opinions, your eating and even the weather. Try to release this desire for control and exchange it for faith—that everything will always be all right and work out the way it is supposed to.

You will sometimes find yourself with the in-crowd, feeling superior and judging less popular classmates just like you had been judged. Resist that urge mightily—it is a dangerous slope and will eat at your soul.

You always dutifully color within the lines and work tirelessly to make sure you, your assignments, recitals and tests are perfect. Your drive for excellence will serve you well in life. But—and this is very important—if something you do is not perfect, it does not mean you are a failure. Let me repeat this: if something you do is not perfect, it does not mean you are a failure.

Nonetheless, you will sometimes feel depressed and unworthy when things (and you) aren't perfect. What you don't know, and you won't learn until much later, is that things are always perfect in the moment, and you are learning lessons that will strengthen you down the road.

CHAPTER TWO

Becoming the Observer

Once we're aware of our mind's endless chatter and favorite reruns, one of the most powerful things we can do is to simply witness our thoughts. If you like movies or watching television, this might be easy for you, because witnessing is a lot like watching your mind's latest feature playing on the big screen of your brain.

Witnessing our thoughts is the basic instruction for mindfulness and meditation as well. Mindfulness asks us to become acutely aware of something in the present moment. Perhaps it's just looking at our big toe (not the fact that we goofed with the cotton candy nail polish) or a butter-yellow tea rose in the garden (not the fact that we forgot to pull the prickly weed beside it).

Contrary to what a lot of nonmeditators believe, meditation doesn't mean getting rid of your thoughts like a great big flush in the brain, it simply means witnessing your thoughts without judging them when they appear (and they do). In my ten-minute meditation this morning, I was probably "thought-less" for forty-five seconds. The rest of the time, the committee was busy yammering.

Witnessing asks us to just notice without the reproachful voice of judgment. We can say to ourselves, "Oh, look, there's anxiety," and let it go. Not, "Damn it, there're those anxious thoughts again. What's wrong with me? I can't even sit here and not think for two minutes. I wonder if I have an email?"

This is both judgment and some sneaky storytelling. And perhaps the stories are the more detrimental of the two because they perpetuate the pattern.

I've always been struck by the Buddhist parable of the two arrows. It is said that the Buddha once asked a student, "If a person is struck by an arrow, is it painful?" The student answered yes without hesitation. Then the Buddha asked, "If the person is struck by a second arrow, is it even more painful?" I can imagine the student's confused silence until the Buddha explained: "In life, we can't always control the first arrow. However, the second arrow is our reaction to the first. This second arrow is optional."

What this means is that if something painful happens, like a lover leaving, we're hit by the first arrow. Yes, it's going to hurt. But if we're able to pluck out the first arrow and tell ourselves, "Good riddance, I know I'll soon meet someone more in alignment with me," the second arrow stays in the quiver. If we ruminate about the breakup and tell ourselves it was all our fault—that if we were only thinner, or had blonde hair, or perkier boobs, Mr. Perfect wouldn't have left—that's the second arrow (and depending on how many nasty stories you spin, the third, fourth, fifth and sixth arrows). The bottom line is how we interpret events—or the stories we tell ourselves about what happened—in large part determines how we experience them.

Storytelling is as old as Homo sapiens, and is a profound, powerful means of communication and connection. Stories

CHAPTER TWO: BECOMING THE OBSERVER

can be as tender and inspiring as *Winnie-the-Pooh* or as terrifying and immobilizing as *Pet Sematary*. Frankly, I'm convinced there are more of us with Stephen King lurking in our heads than those with A. A. Milne.

While our thoughts and emotions feel so strong, so much a part of us and so permanent, they are really nothing more than patterns—mental, emotional and physical—that have etched grooves in our neural tissues like cross-country ski marks on a well-worn trail. These patterns probably started for what seemed like a good reason (e.g., to keep us safe), at least to our ancestral lizard brain, but chances are they no longer serve us anymore. At all.

The best news is that we weren't born with the patterns; they aren't coded into our DNA. We learned them, and we can unlearn them.

Again, it starts by becoming aware of, and just watching, the shifts of emotions and thoughts that zoom around between our ears. No need to think about it, no need to act yet, just watch.

A zebra is grazing in a small cove. Suddenly, she hears the almost imperceptible rustle of a leaf, sniffs the faintest whiff of danger and goes on high alert. Her finely tuned fight-or-flight instinct kicks in, and she starts running as a lion slinks out of the bushes and begins the pursuit.

Thankfully, our zebra escapes, and minutes later, she is back in stasis, heart rate lowered, grazing in a new field. The zebra doesn't consciously have to "let go" of her stressful experience. She just does.

We, on the other hand, will continue to spend countless hours in a conversation with ourselves about what happened. We return to the scene of the stressor, as if we could affect another outcome, or go back, and this time, say the clever line we thought of afterward. This is us flinging second arrows at ourselves.

Had I been that zebra, my internal conversation wouldn't have subsided when the lion stopped the chase. It would have escalated: "I knew I shouldn't have been eating in that area. My mother warned me about that neighborhood. Boy, that lion got really close. I need to work out more. I almost didn't make it. What if I had died? Is there a zebra heaven? Maybe I need a bucket list. What if I see another lion tomorrow? OMG, these horizontal stripes make my butt look fat. I need to go on a diet. Is that something in the bush? I think I maybe should just find a cave and stay there to be safe."

The Buddhists have a term for this incessant internal chatter: *monkey mind*. And there are indeed moments when my mind feels like it has flying monkeys in it, those frightening beasts who did the Wicked Witch of the West's bidding in *The Wizard of Oz*.

I've learned that the trick is not to fight the flying monkeys, but to try and just witness my thoughts swirl, watch my mind reach into the past and fumble into the future. If I don't fight or latch on to the thoughts or emotions, they pass of their own accord.

In her book *My Stroke of Insight*, Jill Bolte Taylor explains the difference between letting a stressor impact and move through you (kind of like the first arrow).[1] To summarize, when a person has a reaction to something in their environment, there's a ninety-second chemical process that happens in the body; after that, any remaining emotional response is just the person choosing to stay in that emotional loop. Something happens in the external world, and chemicals are flushed through your body, putting it on full alert. It takes about ninety seconds for those chemicals to flush out of the body.

This means that for ninety seconds you can watch the process happening, you can feel it happening, and then you can watch it go away. After that, if you continue to feel fear, anger, and so on, you need to look at the thoughts that are going through your mind—that are restimulating the circuitry—and resulting in you having this physiological response over and over again.

That's the second arrow.

If just being aware and watching our mind do its thing were easy (it isn't), we'd all be enlightened meditation masters (we aren't). Instead, on most days, we're running a series of stories our brains have adopted and held at the ready when the right trigger appears.

Do you ever feel your mind is like some of those homes visited by American Pickers, the History Channel show where two men make a living by visiting cluttered, junky places, hoping to find something valuable? So full of stuff you can't walk through them, much less add something new.

There's the old wooden propeller missing the rest of the model airplane, the rusted, paint-peeling jack-in-the-box that doesn't open anymore, a box of Dewey-Warren campaign buttons.

Oh, and don't forget the gatekeeper, named Bubba, in faded overalls who stares lovingly at his rubbish and tells Mike and Frank: "No way. I can't sell y'all this jack-in-the box—it may not work, but I love it just the same."

Much like we hang on to physical items way past their prime for sentimental reasons, we cling to useless or unhelpful behaviors—not because they serve us but because they're familiar and comfortable. And if your behavior patterns are well ingrained through years or decades of practice, they can feel like a part of your identity. ("I'm just a crabby guy." "I'm just a nervous Nellie.")

Often these patterns can become a problem—maybe your anger is disrupting your relationships, or your social anxiety is preventing you from enjoying life, or procrastination is landing you in the hot seat at work.

So, you decide it's time to change.

But you quickly discover you can't go from a rage-aholic to the Dalai Lama in twenty-four hours. And you can't go from panicking in crowds to being a social butterfly by throwing yourself in the middle of a 300-person cocktail party. And you can't change the procrastination habit by ordering yourself to just sit down and finish the damn project.

Humans are not equipped to embrace sudden and significant change, thanks to the oldest part of our brain—yep, the amygdala again—the part we share with our reptilian ancestors from hundreds of millions of years ago. It's the on-off switch for our fight-flight-freeze response and is wired to see major change as major danger. It often tries to stop us any time we stray out of our normal, safe routines or behavior patterns. The problem is our lizard brain doesn't know the difference between deciding to venture into saber-toothed tiger territory or trying to change a strong pattern of worrying or social anxiety.

Facing them allows me to process the things that need processing. Fleeing means these things will chase me (growing bigger and bigger as time passes) until they get so big, I'm in real danger of being pulled under.

One particularly vexing pattern I struggle with is unworthiness or feeling like I have displeased someone important to me. It surfaced in a big way the other day when a friend wanted to go out, and I needed to work on an urgent project. My friend was displeased with me and was openly critical of my decision to work. I felt put down and quickly skidded right to feeling unworthy—do not stop, do not pass go, do not collect $200. And from there? It was a very short hop to depression. Not that depression was helpful—but off I went anyway, because that's where I go when my worthiness feels threatened. In an unpleasant sort of way, it's safe there, and I can isolate with my emotional hatches battened down, and no one can hurt me.

But all this doesn't mean we have to remain prisoners of our patterns. To make lasting changes, we have to outsmart our lizard brain by taking small steps, sometimes as small as just listening to the story your brain is spinning. Here are a few small steps that have helped me.

Focus on your breath. Your stress hormones jump to attention when your brain is screaming, "Danger." Then your body and your brain start feeding each other. When your body gets all revved up on adrenaline and cortisol, your more advanced brain starts thinking, *Oh, there must be something really wrong for me to feel this way. I wonder what it is.* Then it proceeds to spin scenarios, which in turn, keep your body hyper. The key is to calm the body down, and one of the best, most simple things you can do is to control your breath. There are many different ways of doing this, but the one I've found that works best is to breathe in slowly through your nose and slowly out through your mouth, making your exhale twice as long if you can. That long, slow exhale activates the parasympathetic nervous system, which, like a soothing parent, tells your body, "It's okay. Everything's all right."

Model mindfulness. It can be a healthy antidote for our strong stories and patterns. Mindfulness asks us to do three things:

- **Be purposeful.** Focus on something and really pay attention, like looking right in to your partner's blue eyes when

she's talking, not looking distractedly somewhere in the vicinity of her face while you're thinking about the email that just pissed you off.
- **Be present.** Stay in the now, not five minutes or five years from now, and not somewhere in the recent or distant past. The past and the future exist only in our heads. The present, if we're paying attention, comes to us through all our senses. And boy, is this tough sometimes. I often say I spend so much time in the future I should pay property taxes there.
- **Be Switzerland.** Okay, mindfulness doesn't really ask us to be Switzerland, but it does ask us to be neutral and not judge the dialogue and feelings. Just watch them.

Remember not to feed the monster. When our emotions are so strong, and our desire to lash out equally fierce, that lizard brain can feel more like a Tyrannosaurus rex. But as difficult as it might be to stay still, it's important not to nourish that monster. He'll just get hungrier.

Count to ninety. We don't like to hear that our anger, or frustration, envy, resentment and distress are within our control. It's much easier (and less upsetting for the ego) to blame someone else. But in the end, as Bolte Taylor notes, after ninety seconds, it's a good bet we're the ones stoking the stress fires. So, the old adage about counting to ten was useful, but neuroscience shows us that counting to ninety is a whole lot better.

We try to stay aware and mindful and observe the patterns playing out in our minds and our bodies. We watch, as dispassionately as we can, without resistance or judgment. The feelings pass; the emotions dissipate.

It's like going from the small-town theater that shows the

same movie over and over again, to the megaplex where you have your choice of twenty shows. Don't like what's playing in Theater 1? Leave and head over to the inspirational show in Theater 16.

Witnessing our patterns and stories helps us detach. Witnessing and acknowledging our critical voices help us to detach. And detaching helps us to realize that we are not any of our patterns or stories. We're not our anger. We're not our anxiety. We're not unworthy because we did something imperfectly. We're not the failure the Judge and Chief Critic say we are.

This is incredibly liberating! And yes, it's tough (or maybe unfamiliar is a more empowering word) not to leap into action when we're triggered by someone or something unpleasant—whether we want to leap away because it's emotionally repellant and we need to escape (flight) or leap toward because we feel threatened and need to neutralize the threat (fight). Both actions are helpful in life-or-death situations, like our zebra running from the lion; but honestly, the things that get us spun up on an hourly basis are not of the life-or-death variety.

Sometimes the most difficult advice to follow is to "stay" when we want to act, even if it's mentally. For example, if I'm faced with uncertainty, anxiety gives me a sense of control because, if I am worrying about something, it feels like I'm doing something about the issue (which, clearly, I'm not). But obsessing about something gives it power; detaching removes its power while empowering you.

If we want to do something, we can get curious and ask what our emotions might be doing for us or how they are serving us. But ditch the Judge and the Critic and be very gentle with yourself.

A letter to my forty-year-old self

I wish I could go back and tell you the parable of the arrows, because I know you struggle in a mighty way with those second arrows. Sometimes they seem to come from all directions: the off-putting comment by a coworker, followed closely by the self-induced second arrow of indignation, resentment, irritation. *Why don't I ever stand up for myself, and how does she get away with that?* Or the pants that were suddenly too tight. *Oh God, I'm gaining weight again, what is wrong with me? People will think I'm unattractive.* And on and on.

I know you struggle, and you're beginning to see that a glass or two of wine after work blunts the second arrow's blow—or at least it feels that way. Of course, it really doesn't, but you'll learn that later. And you'll hear someone say, "When you have a problem and take a drink for it, now you have two problems."

Eventually you will learn that it's not all about you. I'm not trying to be mean here, but your coworkers, other drivers, friends, family don't wake up in the morning, look in mirror, and say, "By God, I am going to do my best to ruin Debbie's day." No, they look in the mirror and think about their own issues, and if they happen to criticize you or look cross, it's because they've got their own matinee playing in their heads.

It's okay to feel these uncomfortable feelings. It's okay to feel anxiety and depression and shame. They will not kill you. I repeat: they will not kill you—even if it sure feels like it at the time. It's disempowering, though, to ignore the situation or emotion and expect Chardonnay to make it better. (It never will.)

And you will learn that, dear one.

CHAPTER THREE

Taking a Pause

Viktor Frankl, a concentration camp survivor and author of the landmark book *Man's Search for Meaning*, is often credited with saying: "Between stimulus and response there is a space. In that space is our power to choose our response. In our response lies our growth and our freedom."[2]

That space that is referred to is a pause.

We are the only creatures that have the ability to pause and choose our response to situations. Unfortunately, we often react instead, making a bigger mess out of an already messy situation. Or we hop on whatever vehicle we use for comfort when we're upset, whether that's raging, shopping, smoking or drinking a martini. These are the vehicles that bring us home to our comfort zone. They don't solve the problem or eliminate the pain—they're just a distracting and often agonizing ride right back to the issue that upset us in the first place.

In pausing, we find that we have a choice. In pausing, we find that we don't have to react. In pausing, we learn to discern what requires action.

If it's a saber-toothed tiger licking his chops in front of you at dinnertime, by all means, run. If it's a snide comment, a rude driver or a fight with your mother, you're not at the mercy of your fight-or-flight instincts, no matter how loud they scream at you.

Depending on the trigger, we all have a propensity for wanting to react, to make the worrisome or frightening situation go away. We also know that reacting (acting without contemplation) is not the best choice. But here's where we veer off into unhealthy behaviors.

We're proud of ourselves for not sending a nasty email to a coworker who criticized us in a meeting, but then we stew about it, write an imaginary email over and over, and go have a couple glasses of Scotch or smoke two packs of cigarettes to blunt the anxiety. So, yes, it's good that we paused, but then we certainly took a wrong turn into some unhealthy behaviors, which did nothing to fix the situation. Our critical colleague is still perky and sitting in the next cubical when we come into work with a hangover the next day.

In some cases, we'll pause and decide this trigger doesn't need a response. The issue or the emotion that it prompted will leave on its own. The power of a pause is priceless. Even waiting a second or two before you speak or act can make all the difference. When you stop and hit the mental reset button, it's amazing how your perspective can change.

Once upon a time, there was a young prince who left home to become the ruler of a neighboring kingdom. As he left, his father, the king, told the prince that if he ever needed help, he should put a light in his turret window, and the king would send a special horse and carriage to carry him to safety.

The king also warned the prince that a nasty wizard also lived nearby. So, when the prince put his SOS light in the window, the wizard would also see it and send his own horse and cart, to whisk the prince off to danger.

That scared the young prince. How would he know who sent the help? The king promised him there was a fail-safe. Before climbing into any carriage, the prince should stop and look closely at the horse pulling it. If it was a light-colored horse, that meant his father had sent it to take him to a safe place, but a dark horse meant it was from the evil wizard and would take him to danger.

As time passed, the prince had to deal with a lot of difficult situations, and when he was scared and unsure of himself, he'd trudge up the turret stairs and put a light in the window.

But, most times, being in such a hurry to escape the problems, he ignored his father's advice and forgot to look at the horse that came to get him.

As a result, he often found himself on one rough, agonizing ride after another. After a few of those dangerous rides, a realization hit him: his hurry to escape the pain was causing him as much or more agony as the pain from which he was trying to bolt in the first place.[3]

This wonderful fable from author and teacher Guy Finley shines a light on how we react when things get tough. Do we pounce into familiar, unhealthy patterns, or do we pause?

The familiar pattern leads to action without contemplation. It doesn't solve the problem or eliminate the pain. Instead, it's just a distracting and often agonizing ride right back to the issue that upset us in the first place.

I like to imagine our prince eventually learned to pause, observe his reaction to stress and elect to wait for the light-colored horse. When we do this—when we choose a positive response and don't engage a negative pattern—eventually, the dark horse stops showing up.

So, a pause can be a very powerful choice. Even a split-second mental intermission can help us think about the consequences of an action and avoid doing or saying something we'll mentally flog ourselves over afterward.

Let's take a pause here to make an important distinction. A pause should never be an excuse for inaction. An extended pause can mean we've entered into a state of procrastination or even paralysis, where we pull the covers over our head and hope the anxious action-provoking situation will just go away, and then we'll feel better.

This, too, is the lizard brain at work. Only it's not screaming, "Fight!" or "Flight!" It's whispering, "Freeze, sucker!" Again, the best of intentions from our brain but not the best advice. First, this type of extended inaction stockpiles the emotions inside of us, and until we feel or deal with the situation, they will stay inside and fester. Second, we're relying on the resolution of an external situation to determine our inner peace. That is not only easy to do, but it's also how we learned the world works: I'll be happy when my wife stops nagging. When the boss stops giving me more work. When I get more money. When I get married. When I retire. On and on. And, boy, is this thinking dead wrong. This is paralysis and not a healthy pause.

So how do we pause appropriately and stave off reaction while we wait for the light-colored horse?

Breathe. Again. And again. And again. With intention, depth and expansion. Breathe as if you were trying to get oxygen into your toes. Breathing itself is a healthy pause. For even more calming effects, breathe in through your nose and out of your mouth with a sigh. The act of sighing stimulates the relaxation response in your body.

Pet the lizard. When that fight-or-flight portion of our brain senses a threat and wants you to act like right damn now, what if instead we soothed it, like you might a scared child? "There, there, everything's okay. We're safe. We're protected. All is well." Chances are the noise will subside, sometimes slightly, sometimes completely.

Do the opposite. Is your tendency to freeze and not act? Or is it to act impulsively? Whichever it is, try leaning in the opposite direction temporarily. This act of moving away from our instinctual reaction is in itself a pause while we regroup our presence and peace of mind.

Practice, practice, practice. Take a moment before saying something, even in nonstressful, nonemotional situations. If you think of your stress levels as falling between one (totally Zen) and ten (Tasmanian devil), practice these pauses when you're at levels one to three so the training is available for you when you're starting to sweat at level six. Think of this as interval training that gets you in shape for high-stress pausing.

Play the tape through. This is advice shared by a number of recovery groups to help a person "fast forward" to the consequences of their taking a drink or drug. The idea is that once they imagine a jail cell, or worse, their gravesite, they will realize that the drink or drug is not a good idea. This applies not just to substances but also to myriad situations. Your partner snaps at you for leaving the refrigerator door open again. You want to retort that he always leaves the toilet seat up. A quick zip through that "tape" shows you a protracted (and pointless) argument that lasts three hours, followed by your need to apologize for your part in the mess.

Is it kind? Is it true? Is it necessary? When my mind spitballs retorts to my mouth that can't wait to launch at another person, I ask myself these three questions. Generally, if what I'm going to say doesn't meet at least two of the three criteria, I know I need to put the brakes on my tongue. Otherwise, going back to the "play the tape" tool, I know I'm going to owe an apology at some point.

Knock, knock. Who's there? This is a pause where we try to identify the voices squawking at us from inside our skull. Is it the Perfectionist, telling us we'd better go over that project for the twentieth time because there might be a mistake? Is it the Drama Queen goading us to throw a fit over a snide comment? The other day it was Fear, who wrested control of the steering wheel, hogtied and duct-taped me, and threw me in the truck. Then I remembered, *These voices are not me. I don't have to listen to them. And I surely don't have to let them use my mouth.*

Imagine waking up in the morning and knowing in your core that no matter what happens, you will be calm, centered, peaceful and powerful in the knowledge that you are perfect and enough just the way you are. Nirvana, right? But it's totally possible—once we unwind our limiting belief that we have to quickly react, reorder, control and manipulate our world 24/7—to create the right environment for our happiness. (Even if we get the right players on the right squares, nothing is permanent. We're back to reacting and trying to control things two seconds later. It's exhausting and sucks up way too much energy that could be put to a much better use transforming ourselves.) A pause takes us out of reaction and into thoughtful presence and choice.

Imagine our prince faced with squabbling subjects, a major leak in one of the turrets, a baby dragon stuck in a tree and a neighboring kingdom threatening to invade. Off he trudges to place his handy "help" light in the window, and then goes to wait on the front stoop of the castle. Here come the horses, one after the other, pulling shiny carriages that promise relief from his situation. But the horses are all dark—and so are their solutions.

Our ruler chooses to take a deep breath, and then four more, finding he is suddenly calmer, and his heart isn't racing so much. Then instead of sprinting toward the first dark horse, he remains seated and reminds himself that help will always come at the right time. His wife yells out from the turret, "My liege, you promised to fix this wretched leak. It's getting water all over my Persian rug!" He pauses, feels those needle-sharp retorts beckoning at him from the second dark horse; then pauses again, visualizes his bride's hurt look when he tells her to just fix the leak herself if she's so smart; pauses yet again, and instead responds, "I know it's frustrating, honey, but I've got the castle masonry team coming out today, and we'll get it fixed right up. And if you want another rug, we'll buy one."

Then he lifts his head and sees a white horse trot up, looking at him lovingly.

A letter to my nineteen-year-old self

College was supposed to be different, you thought. A clean slate without the tiresome cliques and judgment of high school peers. And in some ways, it is, but you packed your low self-worth and self-loathing right along with the clothes and dorm decorations you brought to college with you. You thought that if you were a big fish in this small, private-college pond, then suddenly you would be worthy, admired, found to be attractive. So, you got involved, too involved, really, and in trying to control all those things—academics, resident assistant, poetry journal editor—you find yourself unable to control anything, including, and most importantly, yourself.

The weight of your responsibilities is too much, and you see-saw between going claws-out and completely freezing, unable to focus or move forward on what you need to do. It's small things at first, like trying to be universally liked on the dorm floor you lead, and when that doesn't happen, you try to assert your authority or verbally tear down girls behind their backs. Your struggles with eating, which began in high school, blossom fully amid the pressures, and you escape—that pause that doesn't fix the problem—by eating. Those bags of M&M's didn't fix anything, didn't make the problems go away, but for a small moment, you felt in control (even if it was harming yourself).

This won't be the last time you try to escape on a dark horse. But if this letter somehow reaches you through time, know there is hope. It feels like you, your life, will never get better, but it will.

# PART TWO
Action

CHAPTER FOUR

Changing the Story

I have loved reading from the moment I learned how. Before that, I loved being read to: my mom or dad sitting on the edge of my twin bed, or with me in their lap in the family room, holding the fairytale or children's book and reading the same story for the hundredth time. And I was just as captivated and enchanted as if it were the first time.

Along the way, we become our own storytellers—creating narratives that explain and interpret what is happening to us and around us. And depending on the voice, as I mentioned in chapter 2, they can be heartwarming tales (*Winnie-the-Pooh*) or horror stories (*Pet Sematary*).

It's a tough lesson to learn that events, situations, peoples' reactions and so on, are not inherently positive or negative. It's our interpretation of them—the story we tell ourselves about what happened—that makes us judge them as good or bad.

Events and situations aren't good or bad themselves. If that were true, everyone would react the same when it rained (brides ☹, farmers ☺) or when the home team loses another game (fans ☹, opposing team ☺).

Some of our strongest stories involve the magical future of when and if. I will finally be happy: when I weigh 110 pounds, if I get married before I'm thirty, when I get that big promotion. The problem is that what was making us unhappy at the core followed us, kind of like Pig-Pen's cloud of itinerant dirt, right to the scale, down the wedding aisle, and as we moved into the vaunted corner office. To break free, we have to recognize and then challenge the beliefs of when and if.

So, what's the story you're telling yourself about the 110 pounds? Is it that number will suddenly give you self-esteem or you'll become Vogue's sexiest female? I have been there, and sorry, it won't—at least not for more than a few seconds, followed by the crashing realization that something else is wrong.

The world won't suddenly hold a party when you reach that weight. Traffic won't part, the boss won't suddenly be grateful, people won't genuflect in your wake. What's more likely to happen is you step on the scale, the magic 110 number appears and you feel a blast of euphoria. Then when you turn around, you notice your boobs have sagged another inch overnight.

Think of a narrative that runs like background music in your head. Maybe it's "Without makeup, I am hideous." Or, "I will never get married unless I'm (fill in the blank) weight." Or, "If I ever have kids, and if I don't lose that baby weight, my husband will leave me." Or, "Unless I have an impressive job title and paycheck, I am nothing."

Ouch, huh? Almost needs an R rating for nasty language. We likely wouldn't say these things to another person, but we think nothing of replaying these old narratives in our heads 24/7. The Chief Critic and Perfectionist love spinning this stuff.

CHAPTER FOUR: CHANGING THE STORY

The lesson is we don't have to be tied to our stories forever. Yes, when faced with an unpleasant situation or thought, we can spin a narrative around it and make the situation worse. But we have a choice. We can also acknowledge it and let it go. We can choose to create an entirely new narrative. Dropping the story is challenging, because those thoughts, as mentioned before, have etched themselves into our psyche like cross-country ski marks on a well-worn trail. But oh, is it freeing.

Imagine you believe that without an impressive job title and paycheck, you are nothing. You believe that others will look down on you and ridicule you for your failure. Now imagine dropping that belief, because it no longer serves your highest good. In its place, you choose to believe that no matter what your title or paycheck, you are enough. Just as you are. It is possible.

Very early on, I internalized a story that I was "not enough" unless someone else—a teacher, parent, friend, guy, boss—gave me validation of some sort. To gain that validation, I threw all my energy into being a perfectionist and carried around that identity like a badge of honor: the weary, tireless worker who does whatever it takes to get things done perfectly, the put-together executive in her St. John knits, the gourmet cook who prepares a perfect meal—wine matched impeccably to each course.

If I didn't get the validation I expected (needed), I'd run a self-defeating narrative: you'll never be attractive enough; you're not as smart as so-and-so; you're a terrible hostess; you should have worked harder on that project; and on and on.

This all came to a head about a decade ago when I left a company that was on the verge of bankruptcy. It was one of the most difficult things I'd ever gone through. I felt my identity evaporate, since up to that point, my life had pretty much been my business card. And suddenly I didn't have one.

Like many people in the same boat, I held a "poor Debbie" pity party, which no one attended but me. One story that ran nonstop in my head was that if I failed at something, I was worthless. Another story was that without an impressive title and paycheck, I was worthless. Yet another was that if I disappointed someone important to me (e.g., my family or a boss)—you guessed it—I was worthless.

I overflowed with shame and, unable to deal with it head-on, let my flight instinct take over, seeking refuge in wine.

The Perfectionist and Chief Critic were feeding the Evil Storyteller lots of juicy material, and I had no flipping idea I could question any of it. I didn't know I had a choice. Despite the consequences of relying on others to determine my own worth, I was mostly unaware of what I was doing. Even in moments of frightening clarity, I had no idea how to feel worthwhile just as I was. Those who suggested that to me may as well have been speaking an obscure Indian dialect.

But I couldn't learn these lessons until I first exorcised one thing from my life: alcohol. At that point, it had gone from hobby to habit to addiction, and I could not get better, I could not rise, until I eliminated what was holding me down. Once I was on the path of recovery, I was able to accept the job situation, and then started down a whole new path of consulting and freelance writing. I haven't looked back, except in gratitude, because that one event a decade ago has changed my life in a million beautiful ways.

How many times has something painful or challenging happened to you, and when you look back, you realize it was one of the best things that ever happened for you?

CHAPTER FOUR: CHANGING THE STORY

- A job offer that didn't pan out led you to another company where you found a fulfilling career.
- An illness made you take a hard look at your life choices and decide to follow your soul's calling.
- A painful breakup (that you were sure was going to destroy you) freed you up to meet your future spouse.

So perhaps it's not "poor me, poor me," but it's "for me, for me."

Just changing the meaning of the event is a powerful way of getting out of a pattern. Our times of greatest pain can be our times of greatest growth—not something we want to hear when we're in the middle of angst. But if we can remember a similar time when we survived, and if we can at least ask ourselves, "What lesson is this experience trying to teach me?" then we've opened the door for healing.

There is a Taoist story of an old farmer who had worked his crops for many years. One day his horse ran away. Upon hearing the news, his neighbors came to visit. "Such bad luck," they said sympathetically. "Maybe," the farmer replied.

The next morning the horse returned, bringing with it three wild horses. "How wonderful," the neighbors exclaimed. "Maybe," replied the old man.

The following day, his son tried to ride one of the untamed horses, was thrown and broke his leg. The neighbors again came to offer their sympathy on his misfortune. "Maybe," answered the farmer.

The day after, military officials came to the village to draft young men into the army. Seeing that the son's leg was broken, they passed him by. The neighbors congratulated the farmer on how well things had turned out. "Maybe," said the farmer.

The lesson isn't that our stoic farmer didn't care about his son or the horses. It's that he refused to create a story—either good or bad. He saw that events aren't good or bad in and of themselves—that in most situations, it is a blend of both. Put another way, our stories either serve our highest good or they do not.

My husband and I live in an older home on the water that is also right by a four-lane street. When we moved in, we were startled at how much road noise we could hear. So, we replaced the windows and had insulation blown into the attic and into the outside walls. It made no difference. I'd be lying in bed and hear a truck or a Harley, and I'd get a knot of frustration in my solar plexus. And the stories started: "These windows should have fixed the problem. There must be something wrong with them." Or, "This damn house wasn't built properly."

If I run these stories, I am an inner storm of resentments and agitation, in which my mind is preoccupied with what's wrong, how I need to control and fix it, and when that proves difficult or impossible, I feel powerless, which leads to paralysis. These are dangerous roads for me to travel alone.

Fortunately, in this case, an older story I have is stronger. During the hot summers when I was young, I would lie in bed at night with the window open and listen to the distant road noise of tires going over the concrete main road a half a mile away. To me, that sound meant freedom. I would fall asleep dreaming of where wheels would eventually take me.

At that time, I had no idea I was creating a story—one that served my highest good. Decades later, I can use that story to reframe my experience with traffic noise. Now, if I run that story, I am at peace.

Sound familiar? Maybe you go on a date, and the other person doesn't seem interested in you. Or, a client is stoic and doesn't seem to warm up to you, and you make the discomfort and disinterest about you.

CHAPTER FOUR: CHANGING THE STORY

"My date last night should have been perfect—we have so much in common. But he seemed bored. Kept checking his phone. It's me. He didn't find me attractive. I knew I should have Botoxed those crow's feet. I was too quiet. I should have been more conversational. My blouse was all wrong. Not enough cleavage." And you decide this is further proof that you're not attractive and will never find a husband.

Or, "That was the best work I've ever done. But the client barely said thank-you. They must have found something wrong. What did I miss? They don't like me. Now they'll be looking for another agency. I'll lose the account. I may lose my job!" You stir yourself into an agitated state of fear, and before long, you're so panicked about not having enough money when you retire that you yell at the kids for leaving the lights on.

And on and on. Before long, we've lost confidence, and we've become hopeless and depressed.

But what if we were to stop the story before it got rolling? Instead of the long-drawn-out self-flagellation, the conversation goes something like this: "I expected my date last night to go much differently, given our common interests. But I just didn't feel any alignment with him. Time to move on." Or, "I know I did a great job on that project. Not sure what was going on with the client that day. If I need to follow up, I will, but in the meantime, I'm going to continue to expect future work, which I will execute with my usual impeccable standards."

Period, end of story (literally). Doesn't that feel different? More freeing?

So, when the voices in your head start talking smack, what can you do?

Get to work. I've found Byron Katie's The Work[4] to be effective at stopping a negative story in its tracks. Her groundbreaking process has helped millions of people push through limiting thought patterns and behaviors. And it's simple. When a negative thought or story comes up, she asks us to challenge it with four questions:

- **Is this true?** Most times, my Evil Storyteller will just dig his heels in and say, "Well, yeah, it is because blah, blah, blah."
- **Can you absolutely know it's true?** This second question usually causes skid marks, as the storyteller gets stopped in his tracks because the negative story is almost never 100 percent true.
- **What happens when you believe that thought?** Here's where you can begin to disidentify with the thought and regard it as a separate thing that's causing an effect on you, like raging anger or immense sadness.
- **Who would you be without the thought?** This question moves you further from the clutches of the thought and into a better place. Byron Katie asks us to imagine ourselves in the midst of the story or situation without believing the thought. How would we feel if we didn't—or couldn't—think the thought or spin the stressful story? And finally, the real kicker: Do you prefer life with or without the story? Which is more peaceful?

Get up and walk away. Realize you're not straightjacketed into a front row seat—you can get up and leave the theater. In doing so, we begin to recognize we aren't the story; the story is separate from us—a narrative that we've created and put on a loop in our head. When we think we are the story, and it's a negative one, it can pull us into helplessness, stuckness, anxiety and depression.

Talk back. Yes, this is one instance where you don't have to listen to your parents. Get sassy. Question the story. Put it on the witness stand. Ask for proof. And be relentless, just as it's been to you.

Pick up *Winnie-the-Pooh*. Well, not literally. But when we try to unravel or unlearn a pattern, there can be an empty space, like those empty cross-country ski tracks just beckoning for us to relax and slide into their grooves. The answer is to slide over to a more positive story. Louise Hay, the godmother of affirmations, taught this so well. If you're upset about your figure, try saying, "I am beautiful just as I am." At first, it will feel icky in your mouth, like chewing on cilantro and dirt. You'll want to spit the words out. But keep doing it. And maybe a week or a month or a year later, you'll find yourself beginning to believe it.

The tiresome dialogue that my worthiness is dependent on external validation is a very old, very strong belief pattern that requires continual work on my part. I'd love to say that so many years of personal growth have taught me to burn that particular book, but I haven't. Yet.

I keep working on it because I need to get rid of that nonsensical story to be free.

It's really tough work to realize we're not our stories. It's even a greater challenge to change them, especially if they've been looping in our heads for decades. It takes awareness to notice when we've automatically started a story, especially right when something happens. It takes mindfulness to confirm that we are not our stories; they're just imaginative patterns that we created to fill a need (like to protect ourselves) at some point in our past. It takes courage to be curious and willing to ask some hard questions, like, "Is this 100 percent true?"

Our beloved children's books may have had the same

ending each and every time, but our internal stories don't need to. We can develop a kinder, gentler storyteller voice—that of our highest, wisest self, which tends to be quieter and harder to hear over all the racket the others are making. But that voice is there. We just need to find a way to quiet the cranky committee and listen.

A letter to my eleven-year-old self

I honor your love of stories; all that reading will serve you very well in the years to come. You have an incredible imagination, which allows you to pretend and to write stories in your head. But that same imagination, that same storyteller, can also be scary, and it seems to take over your thoughts and feelings. What you will learn much later is this storyteller is not you and doesn't have power over you. It is just a pattern or narrative that you'll tell yourself when something unfamiliar or threatening comes your way.

Remember when Mommy and Daddy said, "Don't talk back to me"? Down the road, you'll have various teachers and professors who say the same thing, only it'll be more like, "Don't challenge me." You internalize these instructions well, dear one. Too well. And you're often afraid to question others, and instead you focus on how to please them so you can be validated.

And that's great, as long as the validation is there, you can tell yourself positive stories: that you're smart and a good girl, a good student, a good friend. But when the validation isn't there, the stories get darker, and you'll grow up not questioning them, especially the negative ones—that you're not attractive enough, not thin enough, not smart enough. Not enough, period.

So, I now give you permission to talk back. Question those stories. Sass that storyteller. Tell her these tales are not true and probably haven't ever been. I know it's scary to stand your ground, but please know this: leaning into your fears is the only way to dissolve them so they lose power over you.

And then you will know freedom.

CHAPTER FIVE

Trusting Your Intuition

Gut instinct. Inner wisdom. That still, small voice. Conscience. Whatever we call it, it's most likely we've heard or felt it before, often when faced with a big decision. We either listened to it, or we didn't, the former leading to a good outcome, the latter not so much.

In a way, intuition is like our internal traffic light: a green feeling means we should move forward; yellow, proceed with caution; red, you need to stop or things will get messy, fast.

When I look back at the most difficult and pivotal points in my life, intuition was responsible for my saying "yes" to change—even if I didn't want to. And I have learned (in many instances the hard way) that when my intuition tugs at me, I need to listen.

That wasn't always the case. Like many people, when faced with a decision, my default was to ask others what they thought I should do. That was part fear that if I made the decision and it was a wrong one, I was to blame. It was also part not enoughness—believing others were a better judge than I of what was best for me.

I was reminded of this yesterday, listening to a friend talk about change. Powerful change. The kind that picks up your life and redirects it, like a tornado picking up a car and setting it down on an entirely different freeway, seven miles away. While it may be triggered by an external event, transformational change always starts from within, whispered into consciousness by that quiet voice that tells us it's time to grow, go to the next level, live our purpose.

The right path doesn't necessarily equal the easy route. Sometimes the right thing to do is the most terrifying option. It's like we're at the door to the next phase of our life, and our heart is telling us, "Walk through," but our head is conjuring up all manner of monsters and misery on the other side.

We all face these doors. They might be the "leaving an unfulfilling job" door, or "letting go of a bad habit" door or "leaving an abusive relationship" door.

Some people listen to their heart, get the message the first time, turn the doorknob and move through. Some of us walk up to the door, knowing it's the right thing to do, but then listen to the misguidance from our small self who wants nothing to do with change. So, we move on and ignore intuition's pull.

But if the change is necessary to our soul's growth, and we continue to avoid the door, the Universe will drop-kick us there until we get the message.

The obvious question is: Why do we resist? One reason is because, given the choice between certainty (the familiar) and uncertainty (change), most of us will choose certainty—even if that means continuing to muck around in a painful situation and rationalize why it's safer to stay there.

But a more empowering question is How do we get ourselves to open the door and walk through? I think the answer there is faith and trust—that no matter what happens, we'll get through it. And, at least from my experience, life has always been extraordinarily better on the other side. Always.

For me, intuition is primarily a visceral feeling that has been strongest during periods of pain just prior to a leap of growth. I can look back on my life and tick off many, many instances where intuition was so loud that I took action; however, in some of those cases, I didn't act without strong resistance and a lot more pain.

We masterfully learned our facts and figures growing up, but where was the lesson on intuition? Who—if anyone—was supposed to teach us to heed those pulsing feelings in our gut? And how do we learn to listen?

My intuition, which I think of as the voice of my higher self, has guided me in my career and in my closest relationships—the amazing and the awful. I have learned painful lessons about not listening to it, and beautiful lessons when I did. My inner wisdom has led me to my wonderful home on the water, to close friends, my coach, my editor, books, yoga—all of which are part of my support tribe today. I feel much more tuned-in to my intuition at this point in my life, but it wasn't always the case.

Take the case of the abusive relationship from decades ago.

What happens when you take a young woman with very little self-esteem, who believes she is not enough unless other people acknowledge her as attractive and worthy, and you pair her with a wealthy man who seems well put together on the surface, but is in fact mean, controlling and abusive? (Oh, and absolutely dependent on his mother, to whom he acts entitled and is equally abusive.)

The words *flaming disaster* come to mind.

I was his Pygmalion project: a fairly attractive but slightly overweight woman with a middle-class upbringing, who dressed nicely but in modestly priced clothing. He roped me into his orbit by courting me, making me laugh and making me feel desirable. Once my world thoroughly revolved around him, he ridiculed my clothes, told me I was fat, that I had no class, and no matter what I did, it wasn't good enough. I believed him. "He must be right because he's rich and classy and successful," the Chief Critic said.

As I tried harder and harder to please him, he just got worse and worse. Still, I couldn't leave because I had a rabid need for his validation. The red light was on, and shining brightly: *This is unhealthy for me, and I need to stand up and leave.* But I kept thinking if I just lost a few more pounds or dressed differently, I could unlock the mystery of his erratic approval. There were times I just wanted to die. I prayed for a way out.

Within forty-eight hours of my most fervent prayer, a job in my chosen field came up in Detroit, and for reasons that were then a mystery to me (but now I recognize that whisper of intuition), I drove there to interview without telling him because I knew he would throw a fit. I got the job; he did throw a fit; but said he loved me, and I moved away anyway. Complete and utter divine intervention at work.

Despite the divine nudge, I still couldn't let go. The relationship continued long distance, and even though I wasn't exposed to his mood swings and verbal abuse on a daily basis, our phone calls and twice a month visits left me feeling raw and depleted. Plus, now I had another worry: because I was no longer there to keep an eye on him, I imagined him engaging in relationships with other women (which he did). Eventually I hit bottom and said "enough." But, still convinced (more than ever) that I was worthless, I belly flopped into the worst depression of my life. Thank goodness for the new job, new friends and a short-term prescription of Prozac.

This was a first-class example of ignoring my intuition. I disregarded its red light—his cheating on top of abuse on top of admonitions of friends and family telling me to leave him—until I got drop-kicked into change.

There are some beautiful green-light examples too.

A few years later, intuition led me to go on a date with another man, even though my inner judge was throwing up all sorts of roadblocks: "He's too young for you." "What will people think?" But I had a feeling, just a soft flutter at first, so I prayed about it, and intuition nudged me into yes. We went on a date, had a lovely time, and eighteen months later we were married. That was almost 25 years ago. I am forever grateful I listened to that whisper.

Many years later, I heard the same yes, and this time I didn't hesitate. It was November 7, 2016. I was, well, a bit cross, driving forty-five minutes to look at a house for sale that my husband and I had driven by two days before. My husband wanted to move to the east side of Detroit to be by the water. I was defensively comfortable in my current routine and life on the west side of Detroit. We had seen the "For Sale" sign on this home, and weary of my verbally pooping on all the houses we had looked at so far, my husband suggested that I look at this one first, and if it passed my critical sniff test, then he would take a look.

I drove up the driveway and walked up to the front door. As the owner came to answer the door, I could look through and see the wide-open expanse of the lake. As I walked through the home, my whole body began to tingle, especially my hands.

Immediately, I knew this was home. I texted my husband to come look at it right away, and I drove home, my whole body feeling like it was electrically charged. I had never felt anything like it before. Later I would describe this feeling as if "every cell in my body were clapping." It was the most intense intuitive hit I think I've ever felt.

My husband and I talked about the house later, and talked ourselves right out of making an offer. We had a handful of left-brain reasons not to move forward. Yet despite the logic behind our well-reasoned decision, we went to bed uneasy. The next morning, we got up, looked at each other and agreed we needed to put in an offer—this particular decision couldn't be made on logic and reason alone. Within two days, we had a signed purchase agreement.

While we needed to do quite a bit of home repairs as well as decorating, the Universe had our backs the whole time, bringing the right people into our life to solve any challenges. We even received unexpected checks at times when we were worrying about finances. These experiences confirmed that our intuition had led us in the right direction.

Not once did I look back, nor did I cry or regret leaving our old home. We had found our dream home and that was that, thanks to the insistent fluttering of my intuition that wouldn't take no for an answer.

I think all of us "hear" that still, small voice of intuition differently. I tend to feel it viscerally, as a pulsing feeling in my solar plexus. (Interesting side fact: there are more than 100 million neurons residing in our gut, which many neuroscientists refer to as the "second brain.") I also have felt intuition as pressure on my shoulders, almost as if something were guiding me, and a pulsing in my tailbone.

These days, I am more aware when intuition is talking to me through my body. But that hasn't always been the case.

There are many tricky ways we don't tap into our

intuition—most of them spun up by that scared part of our brain (the amygdala) that tries to avoid change at any cost. We slink into denial: "He's not that bad. He really doesn't mean what he says." "What's one more glass or two of wine? It won't hurt me. The French drink wine all day long, and it's not a problem." The problem—or one of the myriad problems—with denial, of course, is that eventually we begin to believe our own stories.

"If I were just ten pounds thinner or more beautiful or sexier, he wouldn't treat me like this." We make ourselves the problem instead of recognizing we have very little to do with it. Decades later, I can see so clearly that Mr. Not So Wonderful's narcissistic, abusive behavior was his problem and had very little to do with who I was or what I did.

"Change equals danger, danger." And let's not forget the good old "I can't leave/stop because I will die if I do" story breathlessly told to us by that part of our brain that hates change and would rather we stay stuck in familiar misery than venture into the new territory of healing and recovery. That fight-or-flight voice can be mighty strident, and unless you can calm it down, intuition can be as hard to hear as a child's voice in the middle of an AC/DC concert.

So, what does work? It's interesting that no matter whether I'm working through a major problem (abusive boyfriend) or a major leap (future husband), there are some common steps.

Get quiet. As I shared earlier, intuition had been giving me jabs and nudges the whole time I was in an abusive relationship, but I completely ignored them. One day, after he had lashed out at me with his usual barrage of verbal abuse—you're fat, worthless, ugly and so on—I fled back to my apartment, ashamed and devastated to the point where I was thinking if this was what life was like, I sure didn't want to live. I remember lying on my bed in the afternoon sun. I didn't want to talk to my family, I didn't want to talk to my friends. I didn't want to talk to anyone. But in the quiet space, I had the thought, "You can talk to God."

Ask for help. Pray—for an answer, an opportunity, a sign. That particular day, I was moved to get off the bed, get on my knees and say aloud, "God, please help me. Get me out of this situation." Little did I know how powerful that little prayer would be. I've said similar prayers many times since, along with countless other versions—all usually acknowledging that I would prefer the Universe to "drive" while I sit quietly, trying not to be a backseat driver.

Pay attention. Intuition is like the soft-spoken, wise student in a room full of rowdy second-graders throwing mashed potatoes at each other. When intuition raises its hand, call on it and listen. Its voice will get stronger and more compelling. The food fight might even stop. It's that powerful.

Say yes to what comes. When the Universe sends you a strong hit through your intuition, for the love of all things holy, say yes. When I got the interview offer in Detroit, I remember a moment of panic, thinking, "What should I do?" But my intuition barely gave me a choice. It damn near drop-kicked me into yes. And when I was offered the job, I knew in my gut that yes was the only answer.

Stand in your power and make the move. In the span of four weeks, the Universe had gracefully lifted me out of a dangerous situation and set me down in the middle of a promising, new life. It was like Dorothy being set down into the Technicolor world of Oz. If that's not a sign I was being watched over and guided, I don't know what is.

Get back on course, even if you veer off. I wish I could say that was the end, and the princess finally escaped from the evil man, but it wasn't. Despite intuition's continued whispering, it took another ten months of pain, trying to control him, failing and finally getting sick, before I said enough. But I did. I stood up and said, "No more." And when I did that, I was suddenly freed.

When I look back on the other major decisions in my life, I followed the same pattern. When my now-husband first asked me out, I had a minor internal freak-out. He was seven years younger than me and looked eight years younger than that. What would people say? I'd be ridiculed for going out with a youngster.

And yet, there was that whisper in my gut, that still, soft voice that said yes. So I prayed—asked the power I believed in what I should do. I listened for the response. It said yes. So, I did, too, and the rest is almost 25 years of wonderful history.

Years later, when my drinking became a problem, I still felt the voice trying to guide me, but I ignored it—pretended it wasn't there, that I was imagining things, that fear was henpecking me. Yet my intuition never gave up. It pled with me, nagged, and when I finally was sick and tired of being sick and tired, I felt—more than heard—intuition say, "It's time to get help." I listened this time, and have been forever grateful for the life I now have.

I have come to see intuition as my internal guidance system, the voice of my soul. I believe it is always for us and will give us the best route to our highest potential and purpose.

Sometimes, I listened and followed intuition's directions turn by turn. Amazing things happened. I walked away from two soul-crushing work situations, freeing my spirit to do other more important and soul-affirming work. Other times, I ignored the directions, convinced I knew the better way to happiness. In the case of the abusive partner or drinking, I chose a route that took me through pot-holed roads, sinkholes and road closures that eventually left me lying in a ditch.

But no matter where I ended up, that kind, gentle intuition was there to pick me up and softly place me back on the right path. Even in the cases where I didn't listen, my world didn't fall apart; it slowly got better and better.

Intuition is always on call for us. All we need to do is learn to listen and to feel that soft voice. In doing so, we accept that not everything intuition asks us to do will be all butterflies and bonbons. Intuition will often ask us to take difficult steps, like giving up an addiction or leaving an abusive relationship. But these are all steps that lead us toward our highest good.

A letter to my thirty-one-year-old self

For the first time in your life, you called it quits—stopped the chase, paused pursuing romance, stopped trying to force a future husband into existence. And more importantly, you said to yourself, "Enough. If it's meant to be, the right one will come along."

You will learn in the coming years that all your pursuing and agonizing and forcing were in fact a form of resistance. And that decision you just made, to let it be, will help shush that scared part of yourself that believes she will never be enough, never be complete without a husband. It's a relief, isn't it?

You let go, and guess what happened. That adorable guy you've noticed at shows and exhibits just left you a voice mail, asking you to go to a work-related event after Christmas. I know your first reaction is slight panic. Is this a date? But he's so young! If I go, what will people think? They'll make fun of me; think I can't get a man my own age, so I have to resort to robbing the cradle.

Those thoughts spin you up, and I know how close you are to saying, "No, thank you."

But.

There's something else, isn't there? A twinge, a flutter that whispers yes.

So you ask for help, ask the God you believe in at the time to let you know what to do. Yes or no. No or yes.

And then listen—intently and with your whole body.

Years later, that one decision, to pray, to listen to your gut and say yes will change the trajectory of your whole life. In fact, your intuition, which you'll learn is never, ever wrong, will guide you in so many decisions: out of addiction, to a rewarding career, to yoga, to a new home, and so much more. And when you say yes to these things—which serve your highest good—your soul applauds in joy.

CHAPTER SIX

Asking for Help

I got this.
I can handle this.
I don't need any help.

Sound familiar? For most of us, these are our go-to answers when faced with life's inevitable difficulties. And most of the time, we do a darned good job. But sometimes, life zings us a ninety-five mile per hour fastball that leaves us wondering what the hell just happened.

Maybe it's a serious illness. The loss of a job. Or someone you love is struggling. All these things can be totally overwhelming and leave you with a strong desire to crawl into bed, channel your inner grizzly and hibernate for a month . . . or two . . . or twenty. While this escape may bring momentary comfort, all the things that sent you running in the first place—an illness, job search, despondent family member—are still right there when you decide to rejoin civilization.

Asking for help is so difficult for some of us, especially those of us who are fiercely independent and used to doing things on our own because we know they will be done right.

(Hark, is that the Perfectionist piping up?) What's more, we believe that admitting we need help is a supreme sign of weakness. So we hunker down and refuse to reach out to others.

Independence, personal responsibility, reliability, self-sufficiency—they are all great qualities to have in so many areas of our lives. But maintaining the mantra "I don't need help; I should be able to handle this" isn't strength. It's pride—and not the healthy varietal. Plus, self-reliance is utterly insufficient when we're faced with overwhelming challenges or a need to undergo significant change.

So, as distressing as it feels to ask for help, I propose that's exactly what we need to do, and do first: before we struggle, try to control the hell out of a situation, fix somebody or take away a loved one's pain.

To whom or what am I proposing you ask?

Let's clear the spiritual air. This is not a chapter on religion. This isn't a recommendation to believe in a particular god or God. You can believe in the Universe, Buddha, angels, divine intelligence, Jesus, Allah, Tom Selleck, Santa Claus or whatever feels right. The whole point is to choose whatever works for you.

This step requires an admission that we aren't in charge. Admitting we aren't the general manager of the Universe, and that we can't do everything on our own is not weakness. It is not a character flaw. It is not a sign that we are somehow deficient in emotional or mental fortitude. It is awareness and surrender and grace. And in a very strange way, it leads to our being stronger.

For me, it's been a long learning road, but even with my worthiness issues, I've come to believe in a power that is pure love and miracles that helps me become the best person I can be (even when I don't understand the route to get there).

CHAPTER SIX: ASKING FOR HELP

I probably should clarify that it's not that I didn't believe or ask for help growing up. I did—from a God that I was taught was punishing and would have no compunctions about sending me straight to hell if I sassed my parents or slapped my sister. After all, this was the God I knew from my children's Bible (mostly the Old Testament), who, when he was mad, punished with floods, locusts and all sorts of horrible things. And that poor Job, well, I really didn't want to make God mad, or I might get the same treatment.

So, I believed in God and regularly asked for things: "Please help me get an A on my math test." Or, "Please make Kevin like me."

When I was younger and under the influence of this not-so-nice God, I developed little compulsive rituals. One of the strangest ones was blinking when I lay in bed at night. I believed that if I blinked at least 100 times before falling asleep, then I would get what I had asked for and avoid pissing off the bearded dude upstairs.

I spent years searching for the right religion that would fix what ailed my soul and psyche. Catholicism seemed ritualistic and empty. My three months as a born-again Christian made me rigidly judgmental and obnoxious. A trip to the Pentecostal church and its tongue-speaking minions sent me fleeing out the door, worried that they'd be unleashing snakes next. I felt uncomfortable and out of place with the Methodists, who were so darned happy and welcoming.

In no house of God did I find home.

And I never did, until recovery, when my tribe explained to me that I didn't have to believe any of those things or label myself anything—I just had to be willing to acknowledge that there was something more powerful than me out there.

I could have avoided so much anxiety had I believed that a

loving power was there for me, 24/7, no matter what I looked or felt like, no matter whether my prayers were centuries old or ones from the foxhole. No matter whether I blinked compulsively or closed my eyes in surrender and fell asleep.

The shortest prayer you can say is "Please help me," or if you're not feeling particularly polite, "Help me!" In my experience, that prayer is always, always answered. It may not be right away, the bush in your front yard may not start burning, and a biplane won't fly by, writing the answer in red exhaust. But the answer will come. Maybe not on your timetable, but the answer will come.

If after all this, you're not there yet, I get it. After my fling with born-again Christianity, I swung about as far away as you can get, right into the arms of another religion: atheism. I refused to believe that anything was out there, smug in my belief that the Bible was a nice fairy tale, that there was no proof any of it happened or that God even existed.

The only thing I knew for sure was being born-again didn't birth me into a new wonderful life where everyone loved me—I was the same unhappy-with-myself person. Nor did atheism—I was still the same unhappy-with-myself person.

So again, this isn't about us toddling off to synagogue or church on Saturday or Sunday. This really is about setting our ego in the child's seat, and acknowledging that we can use some help and direction as we navigate through life.

In that sense, this whole asking-for-help thing is an ego surrender of sorts. Left to its own devices, my ego will convince me in a nanosecond that I'm Einstein reincarnated and can figure everything out on my own, including how to control every person and situation that come my way. I now realize, at the deepest level, that I can't. But damn, my ego still tries.

I have to surrender, daily, sometimes minute by minute,

CHAPTER SIX: ASKING FOR HELP

when I'm in the middle of something raw and exasperating. But I do it again and again not because I always want to, but because I have to. I can't do this alone—or maybe it's more that I don't want to do this alone.

My belief about a higher power has shapeshifted through the years. At the beginning of recovery, more out of desperation than anything, I used the word God in my prayers. Today, I may still do that, but my lens has widened considerably so I am just as comfortable using the term Universe or Oneness. And sometimes that power, whatever it is, talks to me through other people and what my dear friend Dana calls God shots.

In early recovery, I had hoped that once I got on the God wagon, when I asked for help, I'd get it faster than Amazon Prime same-day delivery. I half-expected our dogwood bush to burn while a deep voice intoned: "Debbie, you should resign from this job and become a hippie." I would have taken that biplane spewing cursive blue smoke: "Call this client right now."

But of course, none of that happened, and I would sit on my couch, wondering just what it was that I was supposed to do next. I had asked for help—politely—and some days all I heard were crickets.

I became very good at asking for assistance, but I came to realize I wasn't so good at listening for the answers.

When we open ourselves up to the notion that we have this unseen power looking out for us, and are willing enough to receive that guidance, it allows for a lot more magic in life. As mentioned in chapter 5, I learned that many times the response comes through intuition. And I continue to be amazed and delighted at all the other ways I receive guidance (although not through burning bushes or skywriting).

Watch out for the God shots. A phone call from a friend

at just the right moment. A chance meeting in an airport 2,000 miles from home. We can casually write these off as coincidences. Now, I choose to see some of them as divine nudges. One of my strangest examples is when I get in my vehicle, and iTunes suddenly will play some inspirational talk by Tony Robbins or Tara Brach or Pema Chödrön that addresses exactly what I'm struggling with at that moment. I have no explanation for this. It's not like I was just listening to iTunes. It does not happen every time. It doesn't happen on a particular schedule. But it's happened enough times to get my attention.

Ask for a sign. Sometimes if I'm really anxious, uncertain or even cross, I will ask the Universe for a sign that it's still there, proof that it's looking out for me. And usually, I ask for a butterfly. That's a pretty big ask during January in Michigan. I did this one winter morning, feeling a bit smug as I asked, thinking there's no way I would see a butterfly during a snowstorm. I sat down at my computer, opened an email from Chico's, and the whole email was about their new butterfly shirt collection, and how they appliqued the butterflies. Ooof. Another time, I was just beginning a project for a new client and was temporarily assigned to an office at their headquarters. I was feeling really uncertain about it and questioning my ability as a professional. Then when I looked up, I saw pink, blue, and purple gel butterflies stuck all over the top of the wall in front of my desk. When I saw those, I knew in my heart that everything was going to be all right, and it was.

Open your ears (and your heart). Answers may not always come from your gut or as a sign. Sometimes they come from a friend or a recovery group. Sometimes they're not presented as "this is the answer to your problem," but more likely as an insight you gain from someone sharing how they dealt with a similar issue. When we can see ourselves in others, when we realize that we're not the only one in the world with this problem, a) it's a huge relief that we aren't somehow defective or hopeless and b) without that stress, we're freer to see solutions that have been there the whole time.

There was a time in my life when I believed that asking for help—whether from a friend, coworker, or a God—was a complete admission of weakness, ineptitude and failure. This belief did not serve me well, and learning that lesson was a hard one in humility.

I've learned that the answers do come. Maybe not as quickly as a text or tweet, but they come. As Tony Robbins often says, "God's delays are not God's denials."

Asking for help is not just about getting answers; it's about the act of asking. Something happens to us when we become vulnerable and ask for help from someone or something. It softens us. It lets us connect with other human beings who find joy in being able to contribute by helping others. It allows us to relax into the idea that we are not general manager of the Universe and we don't (and don't need to) have all the solutions.

There are days when I feel like Atlas and Sisyphus combined. And often, my first reaction is to push harder, exert more control and less compassion (especially with myself). Of course, that doesn't work, and when I catch myself in the act, I can remember how tough life is when you think you're general manager of the Universe. I can remember that I do not have to carry these burdens or do this all alone. I can remember all the times that when I asked for help, it came.

A letter to my forty-five-year-old self

Soon will come a pivotal day when you feel so sick that you will call your husband to come home from work and take you to the doctor. You will actually get on your knees and ask God to help you feel better. At the time, you'll add the postscript: "But please don't make me stop drinking wine."

When that moment comes, when you are standing next to the exam table and you feel a presence behind you, and you sense, more than hear, the words, It's time to ask for help, please say yes and do it.

The harder it is to ask for help, the more you need it. This time of your life, this completely out-of-control feeling, this embarrassment, this shame, will end up being a turning point for you. Because you finally asked for help. Not once, but again and again. From God, from the Universe, from people.

Had you not asked for help, I wouldn't be writing this note to you ten years later.

Just the act of asking will strengthen—not weaken—you, and it will become easier to ask for help in the future. Yes, you'll still fuss sometimes, because that "I can do it myself" independence flows strong in you. But that proud sense of personal power is no match for the greater power that has guided and will guide you the rest of your days.

PART THREE
Letting Go

CHAPTER SEVEN

Accepting What Is

God, grant me the serenity to accept the things I cannot change, the courage to change the things I can, and the wisdom to know the difference.

This brilliant little prayer, usually attributed to American theologian Reinhold Niebuhr, graces the beginning of most 12-step meetings and adorns the walls of many a pastor and priest. In four simple lines, it sums up the way to inner peace.

Yet, in my experience, accepting the world "as is" is akin to asking for help: a blow to our ego, which digs in and tells us we don't need anybody, that we are always right. How dare they do that? How dare it rain on our wedding day? How dare our car break down in the middle of rush hour?

In fact, my ego's version of the Serenity Prayer goes something like this:

God, grant me the power
to change the world to meet my expectations,
the ability to resist being changed myself,
and indifference to any wisdom.

Perhaps there are those who are immune to personal storms, peoples' bad behavior, family squabbles, dreams not attained, loves lost. I am not one of those unicorns. But I aspire to be more centered, grounded and less buffeted around by these types of events.

Acceptance paves the way to that aspiration. But it's a bit more complicated than just flipping our hair and saying "whatever" to life.

At first, one of the issues I had with acceptance was that it felt very passive—like I was being asked to just lie there and take life on the chin. But some very wise people helped me understand that acceptance does not mean being a doormat for other people. It does not mean we let people mistreat us. It does not mean staying in an abusive relationship. It does not mean letting ourselves off the hook with harmful behaviors like overeating or drinking too much.

There are so many definitions of acceptance it would be impossible to list them here. But I've come to understand acceptance as allowing what is to be what is. Without resistance. Without spinning a story about why it's right or wrong.

And I think we move through acceptance in stages.

In the first stage, we are in complete resistance to reality. Resistance is a strong pattern in most of us—it's emotional quicksand that will keep us mired in difficulty unless we are willing to change. As the old saying—which I first heard from Tony Robbins—goes, "What we resist persists." So, if we are looking for the blessing of acceptance, the first thing we need to do is release our resistance.

This leads to the next stage, which is to acknowledge the situation more objectively, admitting that something happened, or someone said something we didn't like, or a bird pooped on our clean car.

Next, we begin to allow the situation to be what it is. Yep, the bird pooped on our car, which we just spent fourteen dollars to wash. It happened. We don't need to crank up the stories about how horrible it was, how there should be a net around the car wash, how this always happens to us, how those damn pigeons should be outlawed, and on and on and on. Pretty soon, you've got a great pity party going for one. And the bird poop is still on your windshield.

We then move to awareness and insight, where we can ask ourselves, "What are the lessons here? What can I learn from this experience?" Maybe it's to let go of an insult—to remind ourselves that what people say and how they say it says more about what they're going through than anything to do with us.

Finally, we can embrace the situation with gratitude—the highest form of acceptance I know.

I've gone through all these stages at different times and have spent too much time in resistance. But I have also felt the joy of embracing something that at one time was too difficult to even acknowledge.

Acceptance is absolutely key if we are to move forward. Alcoholics cannot recover if they do not accept their alcoholism and powerlessness over their potion of choice. People unhappy with their bodies won't likely make lasting changes unless they accept themselves first—every roll, every wrinkle, every saggy rear end. People unhappy with their partners, their jobs, their coworkers, other drivers, the lady on the bus with too much perfume, won't likely find peace until they accept those things first.

Buddhist nun Pema Chödrön often relates a parable from Shantideva, an eighth-century Buddhist monk, that talks about our futile efforts to resist our external circumstances.[5]

You're convinced it's a lousy world, Chödrön says, and describes it as walking barefooted through life across blazing hot sand or across cut glass. You know it hurts—it's too sharp, it's too hot, it's too painful. And then you think, *Aha, I have a great idea. I'm just going to cover the whole world—everywhere I go—with leather.*

It sounds crazy, but that's exactly what we do when we think, *I'd like to get rid of him and her and her, and men who wear too much cologne, and irritating people, and drivers who go too slow in the left lane. And then I will be a happy, content person.*

We think if we just get rid of these things that trouble us, the pain will go away. But if we simply wrap the leather around our own feet, if we accept situations as they are, if we accept people as they are rather than try desperately to change everything on the outside, then we can begin to find peace.

It's easy to live our life in a constant state of resistance, where nothing outside of us meets our expectations or high standards. I seem to have been born with a personal obligation to fix everything myself and have spent most of my life trying to control myself, other people, situations, outcomes. And dammit, it's a big job.

In her book *How to Train a Wild Elephant*, Jan Chozen Bays writes, "There are few things more absurd than the notion, 'If I could arrange things—and people—to be just as I want them, then I would be happy.'"[6]

Yet, we gravitate toward staying stuck, preferring to muck around in resistance while we think of a million reasons why things should be different, why we should be something else and why people should behave differently (and I am ready to prescribe exactly how they should behave—just ask me). Unfortunately, that line of thinking gets us nowhere but further in the mental sludge.

I know we're not supposed to spend too much time looking at the rearview mirror, but learning acceptance—to allow the world to be what it was—earlier in life could have saved me so much frustration, grief and heartache.

What might have happened in my vulnerable years if I'd learned to drop the resistance to the line of thinking that made me ashamed and miserable: *I'm not as pretty as her. I'm not as athletic as her. I'm not as bubbly and well-liked as her.*

What might have happened had I accepted and honored myself just as I was? If I had been able to build a foundation of worthiness from the inside out so that when the occasional jeer came my way, it didn't rattle me to the core? What might have happened had I accepted way earlier in the aforementioned abusive relationship that you simply cannot change people, no matter what you do and how hard you try? What might have happened had I accepted that my wine drinking had gone from a hobby to a habit to an addiction a few years earlier?

I just don't know. Clearly, I wouldn't be who I am today. Those experiences sculpted me. They gave me a desire to help people who struggle with what I struggle with. They gave me compassion for those trying to recover from addiction and other unhealthy patterns of behavior. They gave me incredible wisdom about what serves my highest calling and what doesn't.

So, those questions will remain unanswered, and I will continue to move forward, not resisting my past, just allowing it to be what it was. And giving it a full embrace here and there.

One of my most vivid memories of acceptance was in April of 2010. I was lying on the scratchy sheets of my twin bed in a three-patient room at rehab, wondering what the hell had happened to me and believing I would never get through it. I sobbed quietly and began praying to a God I wasn't sure existed, and if it did, I couldn't imagine it had time for me.

That day, I had sat in my first 12-steppish type meeting and listened to the others go around, admit they were alcoholics or addicts, and talk about their drunk-driving episodes, their time in jail or prison, and their felonies. I felt more self-righteous and exonerated by the minute, because after all, none of that had happened to me. When it was my turn, I smugly said, "Hi, I'm Debbie, and sometimes I drink too much Chardonnay."

The looks I got ranged from incredulous to baleful. And I was pretty proud of myself, until the facilitator said, "Then what are you doing here?"

It took about three days of learning—and being humbled—until I could drop my resistance to the A-word and begin to acknowledge that perhaps in some ways it described me. Once that resistance weakened, I could become open to the allowing. And once I got there, I was free. Free to recover. Free to say no to what wasn't good for me. Free to finally become the person I was meant to be. And yes, free to embrace what had happened to me as something that was meant to serve my highest good.

On our sobriety anniversaries, we are asked to stand up and tell the group how we did it. On my eleventh anniversary, I stood up and told the group that I most certainly didn't do it. I stopped resisting and began to allow help, support and love both from my tribe on this journey and the Universe. And more than anything, I am so grateful to be an alcoholic, because without that decision, admission and acceptance, I wouldn't be who I am or where I am today.

The Serenity Prayer reminds us, in so many words, that

we have very little control over our outside life. We do have control over our inside life. It's important to remember this when we're rattled at work, the boss is grumpy, our coworkers are negative, or the vending machine is out of Diet Pepsi. The habitual reaction is to think, Geez, if only he'd be a little more considerate, or they'd stop complaining, or the catering company would check their machines once in a while, I'd be having a good day now. But these thoughts are the red flag that you're trying to "shoe the earth." The answer to angst is not to try to cover the world with leather (control everything and everyone), but to accept the situation and work on our own thoughts and reactions.

- **The boss is grumpy.** Know it's very likely not your fault and compassionately wish him or her peace.
- **Negative coworkers.** Don't engage in the negative energy and walk away (making use of your own "leather shoes").
- **Empty vending machines.** In the larger picture of life, this isn't even a millionth of a pixel. And you have other choices.

It takes a lot of practice, depending on how deeply etched your reactions are. But it is very, very possible to find peace and centeredness in any situation, whether it's to your liking or not. The following steps can help.

Recognize resistance. It's an instinctual neurochemical *Whoa!* when we're confronted with change or something we don't like. Regardless of whether the change is a positive one (leaving an abusive relationship, quitting smoking), the reptilian portion of our brain doesn't like change to begin with and ignites our fight-or-flight system when faced with it. As the saying goes, "Admitting something is half the problem." But we can preface that admission by a question: "Am

I resisting something right now?" Or even show some gentle compassion: "It's okay, this is a tough situation, and anyone would be conflicted/worried/scared/frozen right now." That empathy with ourselves can take the teeth out of resistance and loosen its hold on us.

Acknowledge what's bugging you. Sometimes the act of saying out loud, "I'm really upset at Joe," or "I'm really anxious today," without starting to run a story about Joe or today, is enough acknowledgment. And it's okay, really, to admit that you're emotionally charged up—it is not a sign of weakness. Sometimes getting it out verbally—"My brother is an asshat!"—is enough to stop it from swirling around in your head and causing untold mental arguments with said brother. Author and comedian Kyle Cease is known for his exuberant embracing of all things life—good and bad—with the clause, "And I love that."[7] For example, he might say, "I just got a speeding ticket, and I love that" with the same energy as "I just won the lottery, and I love that." It's his way of accepting what is—no matter what. God bless him for his optimism.

Accept, trust and let go. My three go-to actions when I am struggling with something. As I write this, we are in the midst of the COVID-19 pandemic, and we are quarantined, uncertain and scared. Our governor is likely to extend our quarantine tomorrow, and I am aggravated. How can she do that? Enough is enough! I should drive to the Capitol and picket! But this train of thought only inflates my resistance and keeps me from moving forward. There's really nothing I can do about her stay-at-home order, so I have two choices: accept, trust and let go; or resist, resent and raise my blood pressure. Put that way, I know what I need to do.

Hop on the superhighway to inner peace. Ah, who wouldn't like a lifetime E-ZPass to this motorway? To get that, we need to take a big leap. We can accept whatever happens without exerting any effort to control it, which to me feels at once freeing and terrifying. (But what if I don't try to make the boss give me that promotion? What if I don't try harder to make him love and respect me?) This doesn't mean we don't work hard or be kind, loving people. It does mean that, after we've done our part, we let go of the result. This step requires a helluva lot of trust that something has our best interest at heart. So, we work at letting go of the outcome, again and again and again. And then again and again some more.

Acceptance begins by disbanding our internal resistance movement—a force that battles reality with a barrage of negative emotions and stories. Lowering our resistance is perhaps the hardest step—but without it, acceptance is impossible. When we've stopped fighting what is, we can move forward into allowing the situation to just be, without spinning a negative story about why it sucks. This brings awareness, clarity and insight, which provide us the chance to view what happened more objectively—without the emotion of resistance—and maybe even question where the lesson might be, or how we can grow from it. Finally, it's very possible to rise to the highest level of acceptance: embracing the situation that we initially resisted.

Having recently retired as general manager of the Universe, it is still difficult for me to not try and force-fit situations, people and life into how I want them to be. When I catch myself getting upset about political officials, friends who post morbid things on Facebook, check-out clerks who talk too much, or six straight days of rain, and I want to get rid of them all, that's the first clue that I'm trying to cover Mother Earth in leather. There's your sign, as they say.

Sometimes I can drop my angst easily, telling myself I am safe, I am protected, and the sun will come out again. Sometimes it's not as easy, and I wear my resistance around like a ratty old sweatshirt with cat-claw marks and spaghetti stains—looks dreadful, but I wear it because it's familiar and comfortable.

But at least now I know I have a choice. And I know that joy waits on the other side.

A letter to my current self

I know you still struggle with acceptance. But, my dear recovering perfectionist, acceptance is not something you master. Because life is constant change, you need to approach acceptance one moment, one agitation, one situation at a time.

You've made so much progress the last few years. You're freeing yourself from old resentments and situations that you've resisted and could not accept, no matter how hard you tried.

You're pausing patterns of resistance even now and recognizing where you can't change something or someone, no matter how much you try. You're refraining from holding extended pity parties, which, at this time in the midst of COVID-19, no one can attend, thanks to the governor's ban on gatherings.

As we trudge our way through this crisis, I know you've felt the pull of resistance and have given in. But you didn't stay—you moved beyond it. And as you glide into the next phase, you'll experience some intuitive insights and self-awareness. Perhaps you—and the world—will even embrace this crisis as the world's big "Reset" button.

In this situation, and always, remember that the Universe has your back, that you are safe, you are protected and you are guided.

CHAPTER EIGHT

Surrendering and Letting Go

There is an old story about two monks who were traveling together. At one point, they came to a river with a strong current. As they prepared to cross the river, they saw a beautiful woman also attempting to cross, but she was afraid of the water and asked them for help.

Without hesitation, the older monk picked up the woman, carried her across the river, placed her gently on the other side and resumed his journey. The junior monk was horrified, given their strict vows forbidding physical contact with women. An hour passed on their journey, and neither monk spoke.

Two more hours went by, then three, with the younger monk growing increasingly agitated. Finally, he blurted out accusingly, "As monks, we are not permitted to touch a woman. How could you carry her on your shoulders?"

The older monk looked at him and replied, "Brother, I set her down on the other side of the river, why are you still carrying her?"[8]

This story is a great reminder of how much we carry around with us. We wouldn't go around lugging a backpack full of stones, but we think nothing of dragging around bitterness, judgment and resentments for years or even decades.

Life serves us an endless buffet of tough experiences—from the mildly irritating to the downright painful—and when we rely on ourselves alone to fix every situation, we bump up against our own limitations. Instead of letting go, we find ourselves gripping, grasping, clinging, clutching. "I can fix this." "Just let me try this." "Let me do it." We analyze and agonize until we're exhausted, but we're no closer to a solution.

Right now, I'm finding that I am in the most need of this chapter as I struggle with a handful of problems that I've mentally surrendered, but then quickly grabbed back, ruminating those familiar refrains of "If only I . . ." "What if I?" and "How can they?" Sigh. So back and forth I go, between anxiety and peace, anxiety and peace, wishing I could spend less time in the former and far more in the latter.

While acceptance is a kind of gentle surrender to the "what is," sometimes we need to go deeper, and let go of the "what was," "what might be," and all the other heavy worries we carry around. That's when we arrive at a point where the only answer, the only route to inner peace, is to surrender and let go. Surrender. Let go.

These are two of the most powerful actions we can take. They can be taken together or alone. Not all letting go requires surrender, but all surrender requires letting go. The one we take depends a lot on the situation we're facing and our state of mind.

If I encounter a cranky store clerk, chances are I'll feel irritated briefly, then without much trouble, let go of the situation and move on with my day. In that case, I'm probably feeling a bit more in control. (I can walk away, maybe tell myself the clerk is having a bad day, and so forth.)

When I am unable or unwilling to let go, when a situation is more overwhelming, I need to go a step further and surrender, which in a sense becomes a tool for making letting go happen. For example, if I'm in a state of panic about whether my business will go bankrupt due to our governor's ongoing closure orders, I am not likely to be able to just let it go, walk away and tell myself the governor is having a bad day. In this situation, I feel out of control, powerless and frightened about my future. If I'm to find peace, I need to surrender the entire situation—governor and all—to the Universe.

The act of surrender requires pretty strong faith—that the power to which you're surrendering is a loving power, has your best interests in mind and is architecting the future to serve your highest good. The act of surrender is also a strong reminder that we are not the general manager of the Universe. We are not the ones at the keyboard or controls or waving the baton to make things happen—in fact, we have zero control over most of what happens.

Once I've fully surrendered, the letting go is all but guaranteed, because at that point, the Universe is driving Miss Debbie, and I'm just along for the ride.

Surrendering, not beating our heads against a wall, not feeling responsible for fixing the world—all are very difficult to let go. But anything we've learned to do, we can unlearn.

Case in point: I met my soulmate only after I surrendered the husband hunt to God, and said, "You're in charge. I'm tired of looking." As *New York Times* bestselling author Gabby Bernstein says in her book *The Universe Has Your Back*, "The moment you embrace your peace within and surrender the outcome is the moment the Universe can truly get to work."⁹ I agree. In fact, I believe that if the Serenity Prayer had a fifth line it would be: "And the faith to surrender it all."

But before I could ever hope to get to surrender, I needed to make peace with the word. I don't know when my first exposure to the word *surrender* was, but it was likely in *The Wizard of Oz* when the Wicked Witch of the West and her smoke-writing broom skywrote, "Surrender Dorothy." The visual was horrifying enough to persuade my six-year-old self that surrender was a dreadful, terrible, very bad thing. And I kept that belief throughout my life, my only other exposure to the word being that of battlefields, when the good guys or the bad guys were cornered enough to give up, and submit to punishment, imprisonment, or worse. Even if I could get beyond the negative implications of the battlefield definition, I struggled with the idea of giving up and letting something I couldn't see, touch, smell or hear take over.

As a perfectionist, I never comprehended or entertained the idea of surrendering and letting go—two suggestions that would have sent me into a manic stage of panic.

Let go? Are you freaking kidding me? What if something goes wrong? What if I allow a person to make a mistake? What if I make a mistake? What if I don't come up with the most creative idea? What if I don't serve the right appetizers? What if it rains? What if the house doesn't look perfect? What if I don't intervene in family squabbles? What if I make the wrong choice? What if I say the wrong thing?

From mundane to major situations, we try and push and agonize, and then push and agonize from a different direction, trying to force the outcome we believe is right.

For years, part of my role in public relations was to plan and host large events, and I enjoyed a reputation as the woman who could execute an exceptional one. And I did. Time and time again. But no one knew the agony that gripped my body from the moment we started planning until the last guest went home.

I drove myself—and everyone—crazy, thinking of every possible thing that could go wrong so we could be prepared for it. I pushed my suppliers to practice again and again and have backup computers for the backup computers. I rehearsed my subject matter experts until they could recite key messages during their REM cycles. I warned against miscues so many times that one of my engineers started calling me Miss Cue. It was hilarious and heartbreaking at the same time.

Yes, a mistake could have caused repercussions to my reputation and, potentially, my career, depending on the magnitude of the event. But the more insidious truth was that, as a perfectionist, a mistake would have meant utter failure, no matter if it was simply an appetizer missing the garnish. Those are things I would toss into my already heavy backpack of disappointments, humiliations and resentments.

How much lighter my life would have been had I known about surrender and letting go. How much more joy I could have experienced. How much more growth and freedom. But like everyone else, I'm on my own path, and I'm grateful that I eventually learned about this tool instead of going through the rest of my life burdened by the weight of every mistake, every personal slight, every painful memory.

So, in life's most agonizing situations, what if we could reframe surrender into something more positive? What if surrender didn't mean giving up, but meant opening up—to whatever is going to happen, knowing all will be well? It can be hard to do this. But the resulting freedom from dropping the rocks out of our backpack is so worth it—and necessary—for our growth and peace.

A few years ago, I took on a big project to help out a client. I had no experience in this particular field, which was finance-related, and my inner critic had a field day: "You're in over your head. You'll fail. You don't know what you're doing. You dealing with numbers? Oh, that's rich."

When a mentor asked me if I'd tried just surrendering this particularly vexing project, I was aghast. *What? I should just sit here and do nothing and wait for the dogwood bush to burst into flames and intone instructions? Mon Dieu! How could that help? Nonsense! I must get busy, work harder, worry more. That is how you make shit happen.*

Thankfully, I have a very patient mentor, who explained that she views surrender as more of a letting go, not giving up. Huh? You mean when I surrender something, I don't have to wave the white flag, throw myself on the ground in a ball and admit defeat? What a valuable reframing this was. It allowed me to humbly acknowledge what wasn't in my control (other people and what they think) and what was in my control: tapping into my inner wisdom, asking for help and taking inspired action.

My mentor then told me—and this is where the epiphany happened—that after I had done my best, I was to let go of the outcome. That was beyond uncomfortable and unnerving. But I did it anyway. And remarkably, in this particular situation, solutions began falling into place like the tumblers in a complex lock, disengaging in succession.

As I wrote earlier, surrendering and letting go are still a big point of work for me. When I initially drafted this book, I was overwhelmed by a very difficult situation involving someone dear to me. For reasons I couldn't fathom, this person had lashed out at me. I was devastated, replaying the interactions over and over and over again in my head and trying to figure out what had happened to make her act this way. I went through every tool in this book, and then some, trying to find some relief. I was like Fred Flintstone wildly rummaging through his hallway closet looking for his bowling ball.

I knew the answer was to surrender, and I did that in my head countless times, asking for help and trying to let go, but that awful interaction kept playing on loop. I started losing my faith in the Universe because the answers weren't coming right away. A friend remarked, "When you put a timetable on your prayers, that's controlling, not surrendering." And just as she said that, a butterfly flew by my window.

Within a month, the answer came—to seek first to understand and then be understood. It completely reframed the way I was looking at the situation. I reached out with love and got love in return. That painful situation is now a memory.

I've used the tools in this book to move through difficulties, but there are a few in particular that help me with letting go.

Park that thought. I've been told that when you have troublesome thoughts, you should let them pass by like clouds in the sky. Perhaps that works if you can't find a convenient parking space when it's raining, but in really agonizing situations, those puffy white things are thunderclouds, and they don't move from their position directly over my head. One thing that has helped, however, is to tell the thoughts that I hear them, and I'll get to them later. Put them in a waiting room, so to speak. It's not a complete letting go, but it's a postponement. This way they know they will get attention, but just not now, as they are demanding.

Box it up. I have a special container I call the God box, but you can call it whatever you like. When I am faced with a problem so big I know I can't solve it, or I've banged my head against the wall so many times, trying to solve it, I will write the problem on a small piece of paper and put it in the box. I think this helps in two ways: one, the act of writing the problem on a piece of paper gets it out of your head; and two, physically putting it in a special place reserved for miracles takes the burden off you.

Reach out. When I was struggling to make sense of the difficult situation I mentioned, the Universe sent a friend to me who had experienced something similar. Listening to her story and what she had learned made me realize I wasn't nuts, I was still a good person, I was still worthy. I began to understand that the best thing to do was leave the other person alone and find peace in not doing anything and not trying to fix anything.

Drop the rocks. Our burdens and worries weigh us down exponentially more than anything we've ever tried to carry. What's worse is that we not only lug around today's problems, but we also carry around those from our past and what might happen in the future. It's exhausting mentally, emotionally and even physically. After the call with my friend, I felt like a hot air balloon just after the sandbags are removed: light, weightless, burdenless.

Somatic surrender. I've had to start looking at surrender in a different way. I was repeatedly surrendering in my head, repeating "I surrender this issue" with the mechanical intonation of a Stepford wife, but that clearly isn't enough. Surrender needs to happen in my body as well as my mind, because when my mind ruminates on anxious feelings, my body is clearly the recipient of the resulting potent cocktail of stress hormones. Through its progressive relaxation technique, yoga nidra helps me to get my body to where I am utterly relaxed and almost lucid. In this state, I can sense an opening in my chest and feel myself express the thought, "I surrender my troubles to you."

There are still moments when I forget I'm not the general manager of the Universe. There are moments when I feel like I and I alone must steer every situation and control every outcome. There are moments when I forget how to surrender. There are moments when I feel like I've forgotten every lesson I've learned. There are moments when no tool in my toolbox assuages my anxiety. There are moments when I feel like the Universe has forgotten me.

But these are just moments—sometimes lots of moments strung together, but still just moments, not forever. When I remember that, I widen my perspective and recall one of life's most important lessons: we must let go of people, places and situations, and let them do and unfold as they should. Our meddling is not required.

What is required is letting go and surrendering wholeheartedly—from our busy minds to our anxious bodies. It also helps to find support along the way, because sharing our problems with someone else helps take the burden off our shoulders, which are already slumped over under the weight of the world. And even in the midst of our darkest moments and paralysis, we can try to remember that our higher power is at work. Things may not, and often will not, happen according to our blueprint or timing, but they happen for our greatest good. And allowing the future to unfold hands-off and with peace in our hearts is the truest form of surrender.

A letter to my future self

I imagine you sometimes, smiling and peaceful, gliding through life. You are fairly unflappable, but when people or situations slide under your skin, you are able to allow them to glide right back out.

I know this strength and resilience is the result of the pain and personal growth you've experienced throughout your life. As the old saying goes, "Our times of pain are our periods of highest growth." Well, sister, I'm really setting you up for success then, because these last few months have been a doozy of difficultness.

In fact, Father Time can have 2020 back and stick it up his nether region, as far as I'm concerned. But I digress.

I imagine you have realized the beautiful art of surrender, and I wish I had that skill now. But what I do know is that I won't master it by wishing. I need to practice surrender. Again and again and again. In both little situations and big problems. And surrendering in both my mind and my body.

Future self, I see you as an expression of grace, and I look forward to becoming you.

CHAPTER NINE

Trusting That Something Better Is Coming

A strip of metal once rested comfortably on a low shelf in a factory. It remained there a long time, collecting dust. One day, a workman picked it up, carried it to a bench and began to twist it out of its usual shape.

"Why are you doing this to me?" shouted the alarmed and frightened piece of metal.

"To enable you to see wonders beyond your imagination," said the workman. "Just now it all seems strange and frightening, but someday you will be very glad. You see, I am turning you into a telescope."[10]

This story from author and teacher Vernon Howard accurately describes how change and uncertainty feel sometimes—like we're being twisted out of our usual shape, and we don't understand why.

Surrender is really difficult without unwavering trust that something better will happen. Surrender without trust is a little like waving a forlorn white flag—feeling like we're done for, and we might as well crawl under the covers and wait for old age to come snag us.

We like to believe that if the Universe is for us, then life will be a certain way. Even if we've surrendered a situation, we tend to feel entitled to certain outcomes. "If I work my tail off, I'll be recognized and well compensated." "If I do things for other people, they will always appreciate and love me back." "If I keep my life neat and organized, I will always avoid anxiety and chaos."

But when these outcomes don't happen, our faith is shaken. It's like opening the Christmas present we hope is the Easy-Bake Oven we asked for, but to our dismay, it's a brown wool sweater. Rats. Maybe there isn't a Santa Claus after all.

This type of all-or-nothing thinking constricts our vision and prevents us from seeing the larger landscape of possibility. It presumes the only right way is our way, and the idea of a different or better outcome simply can't exist in this environment.

There were times in my life that if I heard the cliché, "when one door closes, another one opens," one more time, I swore I would transform into a Tasmanian she-devil and have the person who said it for a late-morning snack. Oh, how I hated that trite phrase. And oh, how I learned that 99.9 percent of the time, it's absolutely true.

Just because an outcome is not the one we want doesn't mean we're on the naughty list or that the Universe is conspiring against us. How many times in life has something happened that was so painful at the time but led to a much better situation? Often, the times of our greatest grief end up being the times of greatest growth. While the process is uncomfortable to go through, like the piece of metal, we do get through it, and are much stronger and more capable on the other side. We need to trust the Universe will penetrate our problem and heal it—and realize it won't necessarily happen on our timetable or in the manner we think is best.

CHAPTER NINE: TRUSTING THAT SOMETHING BETTER IS COMING

During my senior year in college, I was invited to interview for a job at a major auto manufacturer. I flew to Detroit for the interview and left, believing I had impressed the top PR executives with my writing and pedigree from the number-one-rated journalism school. I anxiously awaited the call that would bring good news. My father had worked for the same company, and that, plus my writing skills, made me confident one of the three positions had my name on it. The call came. Only instead of congratulations, the HR manager said, "I'm sorry. You were the runner-up."

I felt myself and my life collapse right then and there on my dormitory bed. I went into complete fight-or-flight mode, fearing that I had no future now that I had failed to get *the* job. I called my parents in shame. I cried. I panicked. I stayed up all night in one of the commons rooms, furiously typing resumes instead of studying for my communications law final the next morning.

Never once did I consider that something better would come of this. My focus was constricted: This was the only job that would work. There were no other opportunities for me. In the entire world. Ever.

Had I had more faith in a God that had my back (and my future) no matter what, my response would have been so different. I would have felt intense disappointment, but then turned a hopeful eye to the future and said, "Well, there's something far better for me out there."

Because there was. I took a job as a reporter for a small city newspaper and cut my writer's teeth covering every manner of news. I even won two Associated Press awards for investigative journalism and feature writing. It was not the career I ended up pursuing, but it was a critical step toward my future.

Have you ever had a similar experience? Maybe you've met

someone who you're sure is Mr. Right. And then something happens, and he leaves. You think, *That's it. I'm destined to be single and lonely the rest of my life because there is no other man out there for me.* Then you happen to meet someone, and, lo and behold, he is amazing and loving and you look back and think, *Thank God that I got rid of the other jerk—if he was still around, I'd have never met the true love of my life.*

We can use these situations as proof points that there is something better on the other side when we get tunnel vision. And ultimately, as much as we don't want to hear it when we're mired in misery, we do have a choice. We can choose to think there's something better already on its way to us, or we can choose to think it's the end of the world. It's a subtle form of manifesting: If, despite how upset we are, we trust that something better is coming, we will likely be happier and more fulfilled than if we just swim in fear, waiting for something awful to transpire.

The subject of manifestation is outside the scope of this book, but we have a choice when change smacks us in the face: we can expect something better to happen or expect something worse. It's back to the stories we tell ourselves, whether we sling second arrows and whether we trust our higher power or not.

Many years later, after a successful career at the same company where I had so wanted to work after college, I faced an even bigger crisis of faith: leaving it. As the company approached bankruptcy, I was given a buyout—there was no job for me going forward. This was also about the time when I began recovery, so on top of the job grief, I was experiencing the additional grief of a divorce from Chardonnay.

I didn't come quietly to change. In fact, there was a long line of claw marks behind me. It was downright difficult to

CHAPTER NINE: TRUSTING THAT SOMETHING BETTER IS COMING

see how anything good was going to happen in the midst of such misery. I was not thinking of how this could benefit me; I was immobilized by resistance and fear.

In any challenging situation, the solution is often in our questions. I could have just stayed there, mired in misery, asking myself over and over, "Why me?" "Why did this happen to me?" "What did I do wrong?"

But to grow, we have to ask the right questions. And these were not the right questions. More empowering questions are, "How can I grow from this?" "How will this benefit me?" "How can I find the door marked 'Change' and walk through?"

Over the intervening years, my growth and ultimate happiness that resulted from the job loss and recovery have often served as good examples of how the Universe had my back. In these two gut-wrenching situations, which I thought I never would get through, something far more wonderful happened. In terms of my career, I started down a whole new path of consulting and freelance writing. In terms of recovery, well, it was one of the best and most impactful decisions I have ever made.

I used these situations multiple times in the following years. A few years ago, my main client had a budget cut, and my job ended in one brief phone call. A major source of income went poof. I panicked for about twenty minutes, started to go into my pattern of fear and "OMG, what will I do?" And then I remembered my faith and told myself, "Something will come up. It always does." Five weeks later, I signed a retainer with another client in a far more satisfying role.

I was able to do this because I believe there is something looking out for us—something that loves us and has our backs—and I mean a loving God, not a punishing one. If we believe in the punishing version, with which many of us were raised, we may spend our whole lives in fear—afraid to make a move in case it's the wrong one and we'll get disciplined by developing hives or being hit by a Prius.

But if we have that foundation of love and trust, we can more easily step out of our comfort zone. Even if we make a mistake, we know we're still loved—that no matter what happens, we'll get through it. And at least from my experience, life has always been extraordinarily better on the other side. Always.

Here are some tools that have helped me get through the most challenging situations, leading me to trust that good things were coming my way—and that I deserved them.

Pull up the past. Here's one instance when it's okay to dredge up unhappy memories if—and only if—you can allow yourself to take a wide-angle look. By doing this you can objectively see how these situations led to something better—that pain is often a precursor to positive growth. If you find yourself ruminating or getting stuck, come back to the present, pronto.

Expect, don't hope. Imagine a situation in which there's a particular outcome you'd like to have happen. Perhaps you interviewed for a dream job. Maybe you met a fabulous man or woman, and you'd like a second date. Now close your eyes and imagine the situation and mentally say, "I hope . . ." and fill in the result you'd like. Now do the same exercise but this time say, "I expect (this result) to happen." Compare how you feel after both statements. Chances are, saying "I expect" made you feel more confident and trusting, while "I hope" left a lot of room for doubt.

Talk nicely to yourself. What do you say to yourself when no one's listening? Do you tell yourself that you're all alone? That nothing ever works out for you? That you are unworthy?

CHAPTER NINE: TRUSTING THAT SOMETHING BETTER IS COMING

Unloved? If our mothers heard the way we talk smack to ourselves, they'd wash our mouths out with Lifebuoy soap. The good news is this chatter is learned. We've done it so long and so convincingly that we believe it's true. It's usually not. Instead of the usual worry and fear, create your own positive self-talk and say it to yourself again and again. And again some more. It needs to get into your body and your nervous system—not just be a rote phrase. One of my favorite affirmations is "I am divinely protected." When I say that to myself—and often out loud—it is difficult not to find peace.

Reaffirm your worthiness. We need to believe in our heart, soul, body and mind that we are worthy of goodness, joy, abundance, success and whatever else we desire to come our way. If we believe we suck at being a good human, it's pretty hard to manifest joy.

It can be hard to surrender fully and believe something better is coming your way when we're in the throes of challenging events. But if you're at the door of surrender and can't quite get yourself to trust, if you can remember a similar time when you survived, then you've opened the door for healing.

Surrendering and trusting in a future we don't know and can't see reminds me a bit of the scene in the third Indiana Jones movie. As Indiana is trying to find the Holy Grail, he confronts a challenge in which he needs to get to the other side of a bottomless chasm. He balks, not knowing how he can cross it, until an ancient and wizened monk tells him there's a bridge over the chasm. Indy looks incredulously at the monk, and says he can't see a bridge. The monk urges Indy to step out into the abyss, and he does, finding footing on an invisible bridge.

That, to me, is faith. That we can step out and be supported, guided, caught, cradled. But before we step out, we have to believe this, that our higher power has our highest good in mind.

A letter to my forty-nine-year-old self

Life is indeed good. You're freelancing now and working out of your home and being paid well to do it. Sometimes you can't believe your luck. Sometimes you even wonder if you deserve such a job.

Then, one sunny September morning, your client calls and says, "This is really a difficult call to make, but we've cut our budget, and we no longer need your services. You'll be paid through the end of this month."

After it sinks in, your gut reaction is one of panic and pure fear. "What happened?" "OMG, there goes my source of income." "They don't like me." "What will I do now?" "What about our retirement?" Your stomach churns and you can feel the fear stoke the adrenaline in your body.

But within an hour, after the adrenaline tapers off, a new, very different feeling comes to you. You remember the times over the past few years when one job ended or a client moved on, something else always came your way. You even use that phrase, "when one door closes, another opens" and smile at yourself while doing so.

Life is indeed more joyful, interesting and intriguing when we relax and allow the good to come our way.

PART FOUR
Maintenance

CHAPTER TEN

Continuing the CALM Journey

In our journey together, we've gone from the Consciousness phase, in which we become aware, observe and pause, to the Action phase, in which we actively change the story, listen to our intuition and ask for help. After taking action, we move into a more passive phase of Letting Go, in which we accept what is, surrender to something greater and trust that we will be taken care of.

In addition to these steps, the Maintenance phase means we turn to them often, either in order or a few at a time, to maintain our peace and serenity. What also has helped me tremendously is creating relationships that push me forward on the path. This could be a dear friend, a coach, a therapist, a support group or your yoga tribe.

I now know this: despite my tendency to want to be alone and solve things myself, sharing my troublesome issues is remarkably healing. I'm not quite sure why that is—perhaps that old adage of a problem shared is a problem halved is indeed true. Regardless, connection is the antidote when we isolate.

I don't get this right all the time. I still judge and worry about being judged. I still feel fear and wish I could pole vault away from it. I have good days and good mornings and good moments. There are days that really, really work.

And there are days when I seem to forget everything I've learned and go slipping down an unhealthy behavior pattern like I'm on the waterslide at the city park. I still struggle with a strong pattern to subsist on external praise.

I always believed peace and happiness were when I achieved x or got over y problem. But I've learned that life doesn't work that way—teachers and lessons keep appearing in our path until we work through them. It doesn't mean we are flawed; it simply means we haven't processed or let go of something.

I hope these tools will help you build a foundation of inner strength so that, if a tornado of trauma blows through or Hurricane Breakup appears, you don't have to claw through the rubble, trying to figure out how to get yourself upright again. You're already there and less shaken than before.

Thank you for traveling this journey with me. I wish you much peace, much serenity and much joy.

Endnotes

1. Jill Bolte Taylor, *My Stroke of Insight: A Brain Scientist's Personal Journey* (Penguin Books, 2009).
2. Viktor Frankl, *Man's Search for Meaning* (Beacon Press, 2006).
3. This is a retelling of a story I found in Guy Finley's *The Essential Laws of Fearless Living: Find the Power to Never Feel Powerless Again* (Red Wheel/Wieser LLC, 2008).
4. Byron Katie, *Loving What Is* (Harmony Books, 2002).
5. While I've rephrased this story, I originally heard it from Pema Chödrön, and it can be found on YouTube (www.youtube.com/watch?v=buTrsK_ZkvA).
6. Jan Chozen Bays, *How to Train a Wild Elephant: And Other Adventures in Mindfulness* (Shambhala, 2011).
7. To read more of Kyle Cease's thoughts on loving what is, check out *I Hope I Screw This Up: How Falling In Love with Your Fears Can Change the World* (Gallery Books, 2017), or go to kylecease.com.
8. While I've rephrased this story, I originally read it in Guy Finley's *The Secret of Letting Go* (Llewellyn Publications, 2007).

9. Gabrielle Bernstein, *The Universe Has Your Back: Transform Fear to Faith* (Hay House, Inc., 2016).
10. While I've rephrased this story, it's from Vernon Howard's *Inspire Yourself* (New Life Foundation, 1975).

Acknowledgments

I am forever grateful to Chandika Devi, my amazing and talented editor, whose guidance turned this book from hope to reality; my husband and my parents for their unending belief in me; my coach Tara Baldwin, who has lovingly guided me on my life's journey; and to the Universe, for always having my back and leading me on the best path forward.

About the Author

Debbie Frakes started off as an award-winning reporter and went on to become a communications executive with more than 25 years of experience in Fortune 500 companies. In her career and all throughout her life, Debbie has been passionate about personal growth—how to become the best version of herself. After reading more than 500 books on everything from positive thinking to quantum manifestation, working with a personal coach and journeying through recovery, she began compiling the wisdom she learned along the way. She lives outside of Detroit, Michigan, with her husband.